RISE of the RAINBOW WARRIORS

Ten Unforgettable Years of
University of Hawai'i Football

RISE
of the
RAINBOW WARRIORS

Ten Unforgettable Years of
University of Hawai'i Football

DICK TOMEY
with Lance Tominaga

WATERMARK
PUBLISHING

© 2017 Watermark Publishing LLC

All rights reserved. No part of this book may be reproduced in any form or by any electronic or mechanical means, including information retrieval systems, without prior written permission from the publisher, except for brief passages quoted in reviews.

ISBN 978-1-935690-94-8

Library of Congress Control Number: 2017949761

Photography from the author's collection, the University of Hawai'i Athletic Department, Brian Derby and the *Honolulu Star-Advertiser*, used with permission.

Design and production
Ingrid Lynch

Watermark Publishing
1000 Bishop St., Suite 806
Honolulu, Hawaii 96813
Toll-free 1-866-900-BOOK
sales@bookshawaii.net
www.bookshawaii.net

Printed in Korea

Dedicated to the real heroes of an unforgettable era in Rainbow Warrior football—the fans. For your loyal and unwavering support, the University of Hawai'i coaches, players and administrators are eternally grateful. This book is also dedicated to my wife, Nanci Kincaid, a wonderfully creative woman and my best friend. I love her very much and am happy to say we are now Papa and Tutu (we're still figuring that out).

Dick Tomey

For Mom and Dad, who took me to almost every UH game of the Dick Tomey era and helped me become a Hawai'i football fan. For my nephews Christian and Griffin—future Rainbow Warriors! And, as always, for Wendy.

Lance Tominaga

CONTENTS

FOREWORD ix
by Ken Niumatalolo

INTRODUCTION 2

Chapter One
BEGINNINGS 5

Chapter Two
MISSION IMPOSSIBLE 14

Chapter Three
THE FIRST SEASON 28

Chapter Four
BUILDING BLOCKS 50

Chapter Five
SLAYING THE GIANTS 64

Chapter Six
THE ONE THAT GOT AWAY 90

Chapter Seven
FAN-TASTIC! 102

Chapter Eight
WHAT WE LEARNED 112

Chapter Nine
BEYOND THE RAINBOW 131

Chapter Ten
CAN IT BE DONE AGAIN? 144

INDEX 150

FOREWORD

My love for Rainbow Warrior football started in 1977 as a young boy selling newspapers at Aloha Stadium. The new, state-of-the-art, 50,000-seat stadium created a wave of pride in Hawai'i. But there was another wave of excitement building in the Islands: the hiring of a new head football coach at the University of Hawai'i—Dick Tomey.

New stadium. New coach. New hope!

Even as a twelve-year-old boy selling lineups, I could feel and sense this explosion of energy for Rainbow Warrior football. On Saturday evenings in the fall, under the beautiful skies of Hālawa Valley, thousands of fans filled the stadium to cheer on the Rainbow Warriors. I rushed to sell my allotted newspapers so I could be granted free admission to the game. Sitting next to the entrance of the locker room and rooting for our beloved home team was the thrill of a lifetime! The deafening roar of the crowd, the sea of ti leaves waved by jubilant fans and the University of Hawai'i band playing "Hawai'i Five-O" are memories that I will never forget.

The Aloha State nearly shut down on Saturdays when the Rainbow Warriors played. The people cheered when we won and mourned when we lost.

This book is not about Dick Tomey, but he's the key figure of this epic time in UH football. He introduced the people of Hawai'i to a new brand of football—a brand founded on love, toughness and effort. It was a philosophy that perfectly mirrored the culture of the Islands. A culture of a fierce Warrior mentality. A culture of love and giving. A culture of humility and hard work.

Coach Tomey felt and understood this unique culture and its people. As majestic as the Hawaiian Islands are, it is the unique blend of the many ethnic groups that make Hawai'i the most beautiful place in the world.

The Rainbow Warrior football team was a diverse group of players made up of local boys from Hawai'i and others from around the Pacific and the U.S. mainland. Local high school players stayed home for the opportunity to play in front of family and friends—and for their love for Coach Tomey. Great players from the mainland—guys like Gary Allen, David Toloumu and Walter Murray—began migrating to the Islands. The coaching staff began recruiting talent from American Samoa, New Zealand, Australia and Canada, and soon other international players were migrating to the 50th State.

Coach built a program founded on the *spirit* of aloha—a love of people. He loved his players, and his players loved him. To this day, any of them will tell you how much they love Coach. He was a *haole* man from the mainland who welcomed us into his home and into his heart. And Hawai'i welcomed him back, with open arms.

Coach Tomey assembled an outstanding group of assistant coaches who were instrumental in the success of Rainbow Warrior football. These were men who were innovative X's-and-O's strategists as well as excellent teachers and recruiters. Our coaches were both demanding and caring.

Rainbow Warrior football was a great source of pride in the Islands, thanks in large part to Coach Tomey's philosophy of toughness. We weren't afraid to play anyone in the country. This philosophy allowed Hawai'i to compete against many storied football programs during this Golden Age of the UH football program, exposing the fans to a national schedule. Joining the Western Athletic Conference in 1979 was cause for even more excitement in the Islands. It upgraded the brand and competition of Rainbow Warrior football.

In 1982, as a senior in high school, I attended a game between Hawai'i and the Nebraska Cornhuskers. I watched in amazement as our Rainbow Warriors battled toe to toe with the nation's third-ranked team. We were actually leading, 16-7, going into the fourth quarter. The Hawai'i fans were in a chaotic frenzy and the players were playing their hearts out. Even though we eventually fell short on the scoreboard, the pride and mental toughness of every Rainbow Warrior player were on full display.

I wasn't a highly recruited player, but I was blessed to receive a full athletic scholarship to attend the University of Hawai'i, where I was privileged to see first-hand how Coach Tomey created his Rainbow Warrior culture. Dick Tomey was not a physically imposing man, but his presence was intimidating, to say the least! He wasn't a screamer or a yeller, but his persona commanded your respect. He put a heavy emphasis on attention to detail. Ball security was a top priority. He demanded your best. He expected you to give all you thought was humanly possible—and then give some more. He coached and preached both physical and mental toughness.

Above all, he created an *'ohana*. Rainbow Warrior football was successful because of this unique culture that Coach Tomey cultivated. He brought players together from all parts of the world, from all walks of life, and made us a family. We all came together as part of Coach Tomey's master plan.

Today, I still love Rainbow Warrior football. I still love Dick Tomey. I have tried to emulate much of the culture of Rainbow Warrior football here at the United States Naval Academy. Love, toughness, discipline and effort are all trademarks of Navy football.

At Annapolis, we call it The Brotherhood.

Foreword

In Honolulu, we call it 'Ohana.

The success that we have been fortunate enough to experience at Navy is because of our culture—one that I learned growing up in Hawai'i. It's a culture I learned from Coach Tomey.

There were many factors that contributed to this explosion of energy that created this Golden Age of Rainbow Warrior football. It was a perfect time, in a perfect place, with perfect people—and the perfect coach!

Kenny Niumatalolo
Head Coach, U.S. Naval Academy
University of Hawai'i quarterback, 1983, 1986-89

INTRODUCTION

"You don't want this, Dick."

It was June 1977, and I was a candidate for the vacant head football coaching position at the University of Hawaiʻi. A colleague of mine was advising me to walk away.

"I know *I* wouldn't do it," he continued. "The timing is awful."

I nodded. His concerns, I knew, were valid. After all, more established coaches had already turned down the job. Besides, what football coach in his right mind would take the reins of a struggling program just weeks before the start of the new season?

There were other obstacles to consider. Because most of the UH assistant coaches had just signed new contracts, I would not have the opportunity to hand-pick my own staff. Spring practice, of course, had already come and gone. And one of the team's top returning players had already packed his bags, anxious to transfer to another school.

I didn't know any of the players. And you can bet that they didn't know who Dick Tomey was. Although I was an assistant coach at UCLA, one of the premier football programs in the country, the Bruins were all about head coach Terry Donahue and future National Football League stars like Wendell Tyler, Randy Cross, Manu Tuiasosopo and Jerry Robinson. The Hawaiʻi sports community, no doubt, responded to my candidacy by uttering Island radio personality Ron Jacobs' nickname: "Who da guy?"

Yet, the more reasons I was given to walk away from this opportunity, the more excited I got.

"You don't want this, Dick."

Oh, yes, I did. Truth be told, I wanted it badly.

In many ways, the UH job was perfect for me. There were plenty of upsides. Obviously, Hawaiʻi was a great place to live. Also, the position presented an invigorating challenge (as you'll see in the following chapters, I *love* challenges) at a convenient time in the program's history. I wasn't a high-profile assistant with a national reputation, and the Hawaiʻi head coaching job seemed like an ideal opportunity for me to prove my worth. I had a chance to make a real impact.

A few days later, on June 16, 1977, UH-Mānoa president Fujio Matsuda announced that I had been named the university's new head football coach. And today, forty years later, I can honestly tell you that my love affair with the Aloha State and the University of Hawai'i has only grown.

Looking back, accepting the Hawai'i coaching job was one of the best decisions of my life. My ten seasons as the program's head coach were stimulating, frustrating, challenging and ever so rewarding. During this time, UH athletics transitioned from an NCAA Division II independent to a Division I school and full-fledged member of the Western Athletic Conference. The crowds for Rainbow Warrior games began to fill 50,000-seat Aloha Stadium. And our football teams began to challenge—and in some instances, conquer—some of the biggest powerhouses in college football.

What began as a job quickly became a cause. The entire state had rallied around UH football, and we were determined to show the world that this tiny island chain in the middle of the Pacific Ocean could be the home of some truly outstanding football.

And I think we accomplished that.

Understand this: This book is not about Dick Tomey. As far as I'm concerned, I'm just a guy who was blessed enough to be a part of a very special chapter in Hawai'i football history. Instead, this book is a celebration of this magical, improbable era of Rainbow Warrior football. It's a tribute to every single player who donned the green and white, and represented their school and state with pride. It's an acknowledgment of the tireless and dedicated coaches who put in the time and effort to build our program. And, perhaps above all, this book is one giant love letter to the incredible fans who supported our teams, win or lose, and turned Rainbow football into *Rainbow Fever*.

Rise of the Rainbow Warriors is the story of an amazing decade of Rainbow Warrior football.

It's about the adrenaline rush of young men storming onto the field with the UH marching band playing "Hawai'i Five-0."

It's about the crowd on one side of Aloha Stadium screaming "RAIN!"—answered by the crowd on the opposite side with "BOWS!"

It's about stadium P.A. announcer Fred Antone informing the crowd, in his trademark, understated, matter-of-fact tone: "Allen with the ball..."

It's about watching game highlights on *The Dick Tomey Show*, hosted by the great Les Keiter.

It's about boiled peanut shells scattered under the seats and handmade streamers fluttering in the Hālawa breeze.

It's about young men from around the globe and all walks of life bonding to Cecilio & Kapono's "Friends."

It's about quarterback sacks, blocked kicks, apples and oranges, and muddle huddles.

It's about a humble local kid from Kailua taking one last jog around the home field, inadvertently starting one of the program's most endearing traditions.

It's about all of the above, and so much more.

In this book, you'll learn how it all came together. You'll relive some of Hawai'i football's greatest victories and most bitter defeats. You'll discover how our rivalry with Brigham Young University served as the impetus to an evolution of the UH offense. And you'll be reacquainted with some of the greatest players in our program's history—Blane Gaison, Falaniko Noga, Jesse Sapolu, Gary Allen and many more—as well as catch up with several former Rainbow Warriors who have gone on to excel both on and off the football field.

My ten years as the head coach of University of Hawai'i football are among the best years of my life. I am excited and honored to be able to share this special time with you.

Aloha,
Dick Tomey

Chapter One

BEGINNINGS

June 1977. Mere days after taking the reins of the University of Hawai'i football program, I was already on a critical mission—an assignment that could have a considerable impact on the very future of the Rainbow Warriors.

It was absolutely imperative that I meet Blane Gaison.

Blane, a talented quarterback who led Kamehameha-Kapālama to consecutive Prep Bowl championships, was coming off a respectable freshman season under my predecessor, Larry Price. But the word we were hearing was that he wasn't happy at UH. In fact, Blane pretty much had his bags packed. He was ready to transfer to Boise State.

Keeping Blane in our program was, as I saw it, Priority No. 1. The problem was, I was having a difficult time setting up a meeting with him. Every time I talked to Blane on the phone, he said he had to "go to the country."

Go to the country? That sounded so far away. What country was he going to?

Finally, one of my assistant coaches set me straight. "Coach," he said, rolling his eyes, "Blane means he's going to Kāne'ohe."

Oh.

Welcome to Hawai'i, silly haole.

Becoming a college head football coach for the first time can be a dizzying experience. As soon as you sign on the dotted line, you're thrust into a whirlwind of activity. First, there's the introductory press conference, where you meet the local media and share your vision for the program. Next, you're shuttled here, there and seemingly everywhere, meeting a parade of players, coaches, politicians, boosters, faculty members, community leaders and business executives.

Finally, after all your public obligations have been met, you're able to catch your breath. You stroll into your new office—or, in my case, a small room tucked away in one corner of a dilapidated Quonset hut. You shut the door, walk behind the desk and park yourself in your chair. Leaning back, you glance around the room and tap your fingers on the armrests. Then you utter the two words that inevitably cross the mind of every rookie head coach.

"What now?"

I remember asking myself that very question. Talking to Blane Gaison was just one of the many things on my "To Do" list. I was taking over a program that had fallen on hard times. The previous season, the team had gone 3-8, and the final two games were demoralizing losses to Oregon State (69-0) and Nebraska (68-3). Coach Price had resigned on May 11, citing "broken promises" and a lack of commitment from the state to properly fund the program. What's more, there were other dissatisfied players on the team, many of whom were ready to follow Blane out the door.

The day after I was introduced as Hawai'i's new head coach, *Honolulu Advertiser* writer Dick Fishback even wondered why I'd taken the job. "Some have predicted a 1-9-1 record for the Bows in 1977," he noted.

I took it all in stride. I hadn't come to Hawai'i wearing a blindfold. I understood that the program faced some obstacles. But I also knew that we could overcome those hurdles. What most saw as challenges, I viewed as opportunities.

Before we go on, I think it's important to recognize that the success of Hawai'i's only collegiate football program didn't start (or end) with Dick Tomey. The Rainbow Warriors have a long and storied tradition of great football. So here's a quick history lesson.

The program began in 1909, two years after the university was established. Then known as the College of Hawai'i Fighting Deans, the team beat McKinley High School, 6-5, in their very first game.

The school changed its name to the University of Hawai'i in 1920. That same year, the football team played its first collegiate opponent, falling to Nevada, 14-0.

The 1924 and 1925 squads were known as the Wonder Teams, as head coach Otto "Proc" Klum guided his charges to perfect 8-0 and 10-0 seasons. During that two-year span, Hawai'i outscored their opponents, 609 to 29. Their spotless campaigns included one-sided shutouts of Colorado, Colorado State and Washington State. (Coach Klum wasn't one to put a leash on his team. The next season, in 1926, Hawai'i walloped the Field Artillery and Healani by identical scores of 101 to zero!)

In 1955, Hawai'i came away with perhaps the program's greatest upset: a 6-0 shocker over the Nebraska Cornhuskers in Lincoln. Midway through the fourth quarter, UH head coach Hank Vasconcellos called "Thirty-one Fly Trap," and fullback Hartwell Freitas plunged over the goal line for the game's only score. Floyd Olds, sports editor of the *Omaha World-Herald*, wrote of the result: "The visitors, instead of being a soft touch, gave the Huskers a painful lesson in blocking, tackling and running. They did everything better, and they didn't let a lack of reserve strength bother them a bit."

Another landmark victory occurred in the opening game of the 1973 season, when Hawaiʻi held off the Washington Huskies, 10-7, at Husky Stadium. UH cornerback Hal Stringert snared three interceptions in that game, including a fourth-down pick that sealed the contest. The next day, the *Seattle Times* noted that the hard-earned triumph "probably represents the largest coconut ever grown on their gridiron tree." (Trust me, I am not making this up!) Their sports editor, Georg N. Meyers, penned a column with the headline, "Never trust a team in aloha shirts."

But perhaps my favorite account of University of Hawaiʻi football dates back to the final game of the 1923 season. The Fighting Deans were locked in a scoreless struggle against Oregon State, the story goes, when a brilliant rainbow appeared over Mōʻiliʻili Field. The home team scored shortly thereafter to secure a 7-0 victory. After that, the local reporters began calling the UH teams "Rainbows." Whenever a rainbow appeared from the Manoa mist over the UH campus, it was said, Hawaiʻi could not lose.

(Looking back on my UH tenure, I have to wonder if a rainbow ever materialized during our teams' clashes with BYU. I'm guessing the answer is "no.")

The great Tommy Kaulukukui starred at the University of Hawaiʻi in the 1930s. He was the first UH athlete to earn All-America honors, and his nickname, "Grass Shack," was bestowed upon him by legendary sportswriter Grantland Rice. In 1935, Tommy returned a kickoff 103 yards for a touchdown against UCLA—a school record that still stands.

You want more names? How about Jeris White, the Radford High School product who became an All-American cornerback at Hawaiʻi and went on to win a Super Bowl ring with the Washington Redskins? Or Don "Spud" Botelho, the do-everything gridiron great—he played quarterback, running back, punter and placekicker—who was on the 1955 team that beat Nebraska and later became a four-time Interscholastic League of Honolulu Coach of the Year? Or running back Larry Sherrer, who in 1971 became the first player in school history to rush for a thousand yards in a single season?

Jim Kalili. Larry Arnold. John Woodcock. Golden Richards. Levi Stanley. Cliff Laboy. Tim Buchanan. Arnold Morgado. Hal Stringert. Alex Kaloi. These are just some of the all-time greats and fan favorites who wore a Rainbow Warrior uniform.

And then there are the head coaches: Otto "Proc" Klum. Eugene "Luke" Gill. Hank Vasconcellos. Jimmy Asato. Dave Holmes. Larry Price.

All of these men represented our Aloha State with great distinction and helped lay the foundation for the Division I era of Hawaiʻi football. And all of them made their mark on the program before I ever got here.

Of course, I don't have to tell you that University of Hawaiʻi football reached even greater heights after I left Hawaiʻi following the 1986 season. From wins over BYU and conference championships to record-setting offenses and the 2007 Sugar Bowl, fans in the Aloha State have had a lot to cheer about in the thirty-one years since my departure. And, of course, there were some real down years as well.

I'll get to all of that in a later chapter.

My path to becoming the eighteenth head coach in UH football history was fortified with hard work, sacrifice, determination, a few lucky breaks and, most of all, the guidance and encouragement of some of the finest mentors an aspiring coach could ever have.

I was born Richard Hastings Tomey on June 20, 1938 in Bloomington, Indiana, the only son of Dale and Lucille Tomey. My father worked for the Indiana Limestone Company, which was founded in 1926 and today remains one of America's largest limestone quarries.

Pop moved the family to Chicago, but our stay there lasted for just two months. The big city life, he decided, wasn't the environment that he wanted my older sister, Marcia, and I to grow up in. We returned to Indiana and lived in a community called Beverly Shores. The following summer we relocated again, this time to Michigan City, a town situated along Lake Michigan, just a short distance from South Bend. (For you trivia buffs, Michigan City is the birthplace of Don Larsen, the New York Yankees great who pitched a perfect game in the 1956 World Series.)

Although I loved sports—I played football, baseball and basketball—I was slow and overweight. All the guys at school called me "Tubby." In the seventh grade, I was cut from my junior high basketball team because of my girth.

"Lose some weight," the coach advised me. "If you do, you'll have a great chance to make the team next year." (That inspired me to shed the extra pounds, and I did make the team the following year.)

My favorite sport was actually baseball, and I still love the game. Whether it was in summer leagues or college pick-up games, I played baseball wherever my coaching career took me. I kid you not, I played competitive baseball in Arizona until I was sixty-seven!

(It's no wonder that, after joining UH in 1977, I became good friends with the school's baseball coach, Les Murakami. That same year, interestingly enough, the baseball Rainbows became the university's first athletic program to top the national rankings. It was also the season that a young freshman pitcher named Derek Tatsuno made his debut for UH. I got to know Derek pretty well. He liked to visit our ticket office, where Edith Tanida and Donna Murayama always had plenty of food!)

Although I was in much better shape than my junior high days, I was still woefully slow. As a result, although I played some quarterback at Elston High in Michigan City, my main position was on the offensive line, as a guard.

After high school, I managed to get accepted to DePauw University, a liberal arts college located in Greencastle, Indiana. I wasn't on an athletic scholarship. (Athletically, no one knew I existed.) But I did play varsity football and baseball for the Tigers.

It was around this time in my life that I decided I might want to be a coach. I had always admired the people who coached me as I was growing up. They coached summer leagues, umpired baseball games and took us to different sporting events. They had such a profound impact on my life that I thought, "Gee, coaching would really be fun."

After graduating from DePauw with a B.A. in Economics, I went to Cape Cod in Massachusetts to play and work at the Ted Williams Baseball Camp. A month into the summer, however, a job opportunity fell through, and I hustled back to Indiana to interview for a coaching job at a junior high school.

Serendipity had entered my life. Looking back, I was so fortunate that my initial job plans fell through.

My very first coaching job was at School 86, a junior high in Indianapolis situated just across the street from Butler University. Butler's athletic director at the time was Tony Hinkle, and he was also the school's football, basketball and baseball coach. He was an amazing leader. Years later, in 1965, Hinkle was inducted into the Naismith Memorial Basketball Hall of Fame as a contributor. Today, Butler's basketball arena is known as the Hinkle Fieldhouse.

I coached football, basketball, and boys and girls track. If School 86 had a baseball program, I probably would have coached that, too. I also taught social studies and supervised both the lunch room and safety patrol. I loved every second of it!

Eventually, I knew, I would have to decide which sport I really wanted to coach. But that could wait.

I did appreciate the unique aspects that football presented. While a basketball team may have a dozen or so players, for example, a high school football coach gets to work with forty, fifty, maybe even a hundred young athletes. In my eyes, that meant having more young men I could mentor and more opportunities to make a meaningful difference.

Football also has three distinct units: offense, defense and special teams. There are many different positions in football, with each position requiring unique skill sets, physical attributes and even personality traits. A wide receiver, for instance, is wired differently from a defensive tackle or linebacker. And, as a head coach, it's your responsibility to bring them all together and form a cohesive team.

I also liked the fact that, with fewer games to play, every football game was important. Early on in my coaching career, I realized that nothing feels quite as satisfying as a winner's locker room in football. (Conversely, of course, few things are as devastating as the loser's locker room. Wait till we get to the BYU chapter!)

In 1962, during my second year at School 86, a man named Hank Johnson walked across the street from Butler to see me. Hank worked with Tony Hinkle as an assistant coach, and I coached Hank's son, Jimmy.

"Have you ever thought about what you want to do as a career?" Hank asked me.

"I'd like to coach," I replied.

"That's why I'm here," he said. "I think you might have a real future in coaching. But what's your next step?"

I wasn't sure what Hank was getting at. I told him that I was happy coaching at School 86.

"That's fine, Dick. But there has to be a next step."

I paused for a moment. "Well, maybe I can go coach at one of the high schools in town," I said. (Clearly, long-term planning was not one of my strengths.)

"You could," he said. "Or maybe you could be a graduate assistant at one of the universities. Say, Miami of Ohio."

Miami of Ohio? I was an Indiana kid, and I'd lived in Indiana practically my entire life. What was Miami of Ohio?

Hank smiled. "Look it up," he said.

So I did. In those days, of course, there was no Internet. It took a trip to the library to find out everything I needed to know about Miami of Ohio.

I learned that the school was widely regarded as a cradle for legendary football coaches. It's where a lot of the greats got started, including Paul Brown, Woody Hayes, Bill Arnsparger, Sid Gillman, Weeb Ewbank, Ara Parseghian and Larry Smith. Three of today's most successful coaches—Jim Tressel, John Harbaugh and Sean Payton—all learned their trade at Miami of Ohio.

With Hank's encouragement, I took a leap of faith and made the three-hour drive to Oxford, Ohio, where the school's main campus was located. At the time, there were no job openings on the coaching staff. Head coach John Pont suggested that I apply for a dormitory advisor position and serve as a volunteer coach on his team. I got the job and worked in a dorm where many of our freshman players lived. For my work, I got free room and board, plus free tuition at the school.

That first year was a huge adjustment. Miami of Ohio was a big-time program with a glorious history. We had an outstanding season, even beating Purdue of the Big Ten conference.

After the season, John—all the coaches at Miami were called by their first names—took a job at Yale. He encouraged me to stay. The new coach, I was told, was going to be some guy who was an assistant at Ohio State.

His name? Glenn Edward Schembechler.

You know him simply as "Bo."

I spent only one and a half years with Bo, but that time with him completely changed my career trajectory. Heck, it changed my life.

Most people saw Bo as this gruff, no-nonsense disciplinarian, and he wore that reputation well. But I also knew him to be a great man with an extraordinary humanity about him. Yes, he could be intense and fiery, but he also had a compassionate and lighthearted side that most folks rarely got to see.

I'll share this story with you to illustrate the kind of man Bo was. That first spring after Bo joined Miami, the RedHawks baseball team was down an assistant coach and, because word got out that I loved baseball, I was offered an opportunity to coach the freshman squad. Now, at this point in time, I hardly knew Bo at all. He had just recently arrived on campus—Miami of Ohio was Bo's alma mater—after establishing a name for himself at mighty Ohio State, and I was just a lowly grad assistant who was green as grass.

I walked into Bo's office with my heart in my hands. I knew this wasn't going to be an easy sell.

"Umm, Coach, the reason I'm here is to ask you if I could coach the freshman baseball team this semester. I would have to miss some of spring practice…"

As you can imagine, that didn't go over very well.

"What the hell do you mean, 'Miss some of spring practice'?" Bo barked incredulously. "I thought you wanted to be a *football* coach!"

"I *do* want to be a football coach, but I also love baseball," I explained. "I love to play it, and I also love coaching it. This is just an opportunity that came up. I know I can make it to football practices and meetings on some days. And I'll do extra work. I'll do whatever it takes."

All the while, I was thinking to myself, "I'm pissing him off, I just know it. I may as well pack my bags right now."

Bo was silent for a moment. Then he shook his head and sighed.

"I tell you what. Let me think about this. You come back tomorrow, and we'll talk some more."

I got up from my chair and walked toward the door. Just as I reached for the doorknob, Bo bellowed, "Tomey! Get your ass back over here and sit down!"

Bo glared at me as I hustled back to his desk. And then, to my complete surprise, he broke into a beautiful, enormous smile.

"You know what, Tomey? We don't know each other very well. And here's something you really don't know about me: I love baseball. Heck, I'm an old left-handed pitcher from Barberton, Ohio. So, yeah, I love baseball just like you do. And when somebody tells me that he has one chance to coach a sport he loves, I understand that. So let's make this work."

Wow. This one moment with Bo changed my perception of him forever. To this day, my eyes start to glisten whenever I recall that conversation.

Bo, of course, went on to become one of the greatest coaches the sport of football has ever known. During his twenty years at the University of Michigan, he led the Wolverines to 194 victories and ten Rose Bowl appearances. He was named Big Ten Coach of the Year six times and, in 1996, was inducted into the College Football Hall of Fame.

I learned so much from Bo. He showed me that a head coach can be tough and compassionate at the same time. And, as I said earlier, Bo had this great humanity about him, and he showed it to his team constantly. The players gave him complete effort because they loved and respected him. Above all, Bo made me understand that the most important thing in football is the relationship between the coaches and players.

I loved coaching for Bo. His frequent mantra—"The Team! The Team! The Team!"—still echoes in my memory.

There was only one time that I didn't take Bo's advice. In 1964, I was ready to move on from Miami. Bo approached me and said, "Tomey, what are you going to do? You know, it's hard to get a coaching job when you're just a graduate assistant. Don't leave Ohio."

But I rejected the idea that there were no opportunities for me. So I sent out 500 letters to see if there were any jobs open. As you can guess, I got a lot of rejections. But my fishing expedition also drew a couple of nibbles.

I landed a job coaching the freshman team at Northern Illinois. The next season, I coached the defensive backs, running backs, quarterbacks and the freshmen team at Davidson College in North Carolina. The head coach there was Homer Smith.

The strange thing about my time at Davidson was that I got fired twice. That first year, I was fired for insubordination after the final game of the season. Homer later brought me back, but the day after my second season ended he took me aside and said, "Let me help you find another job. You're going to be really good, but we just need to part ways."

Looking back on what happened, Homer was right and I was wrong. I had no quarrel with his decision. Later, Homer and I became really good friends, and he was instrumental in my development as a coach. Years later, when I was the head coach at Arizona, Homer was my offensive coordinator for our 1996 and 1997 teams.

My football education continued at the University of Kansas, where I served as the freshmen coach and fundamentals coach for two seasons. Then I became the team's defensive backs coach. The Jayhawks' head coach, Pepper Rodgers, had assembled a great staff that included future head coaches Jack Green (Vanderbilt), Don Fambrough (Kansas), Doug Weaver (Kansas State), John Cooper (Ohio State), Terry Donahue (UCLA) and Dave McClain (Wisconsin).

Four years later, when Pepper took the head coaching job at UCLA, I followed him to Westwood. Then future NFL head coach Dick Vermeil retained me when he took over the UCLA program in 1974.

Quite simply, Dick Vermeil was one of the most driven people I have ever known. He gave everything he had to the game of football. He was so passionate and intense. He got personally involved with every player on the team. Some coaches can't do that. They can't open themselves up to that much intimacy. But Dick could. He would often let his emotions bring him to tears.

Dick was a stickler for preparation and game planning. But the thing about him that most rubbed off on me was his insistence on going the extra mile for his players. He would often bring players to his house, and he demanded that his assistant coaches do the same. I would continue that practice when I got to the University of Hawaiʻi.

There was an adverse side to Dick's passion. In 1983, after seven years as head coach of the NFL's Philadelphia Eagles, Dick retired from the game, citing burnout. The time away served him well. Dick returned to coaching fifteen years later, in 1997, and led the Saint Louis Rams to their first-ever Super Bowl championship. I was so thrilled for him!

Dick's time at UCLA was capped by the Bruins' stunning win over undefeated and No. 1-ranked Ohio State. After he left to take the Eagles job, my good friend Terry Donahue was named the school's new head coach. (I got to interview for the job, but Terry was a great choice.)

Terry and I pretty much grew up together in the coaching profession. We had both worked at Kansas before making our way to Westwood. He was both a great student and a great teacher of the game, and in my opinion he wound up becoming the greatest coach in the history of Bruins football. He still has the most wins in school history (151). Terry was also the first coach in all of college football to win a bowl game in seven consecutive seasons. Ultimately, I don't think Terry got the respect that he deserved. He was one of the game's best.

Altogether, I spent six seasons with the Bruins. In 1976, my final year at UCLA, Terry promoted me to organize the team's defense.

By 1977, I had fifteen full seasons under my belt as an assistant coach. I learned from some of the game's brightest minds. Homer Smith. Pepper Rodgers. Dick Vermeil. Terry Donahue. I gained valuable insights from these great coaches, as well as the many assistant coaches who had served with me.

In addition, my twenty-plus games as head coach of the freshmen teams at Northern Illinois, Davidson, Kansas and UCLA helped me tremendously. I had learned about making game-time decisions, handling personnel matters and communicating with my players.

By this time, I had given a lot of thought to becoming a head coach. I remembered the words of my old friend, Hank Johnson. *There has to be a next step.*

I was ready for the next step.

Chapter Two

MISSION: ~~IM~~POSSIBLE

I was familiar with Hawai'i, having vacationed there and recruited Island players while I was at UCLA.

I loved the place. I mean, think about it. Growing up, my entire world was Indiana. My senses could barely handle Hawai'i. It was breathtaking. I thought, "Wouldn't it be wonderful to live here one day?"

When Coach Price resigned and the Hawai'i coaching job became available, I was immediately interested. The opportunity to become a college football head coach was something I wanted. But to do that job in Hawai'i? Even better!

The UH athletic director was Ray Nagel, who, like me, had a strong connection to UCLA. Ray was a quarterback and halfback for the Bruins in the late 1940s, and later returned to the campus as an assistant coach. Before coming to Hawai'i, Ray spent six years as the A.D. at Washington State before taking the Hawai'i job in 1976. At the time, Hawai'i was an independent Division I program, but under Ray the wheels were put in motion for UH to join the Western Athletic Conference.

Ray and I knew each other, and that was another reason why I was comfortable applying for the job. I knew he would be up front with me.

Other coaches were also under consideration for the position. One of them was Jim Mora, who at the time was the defensive coordinator at the University of Washington. Jim later became known for his time in the pro ranks. He coached the Philadelphia/Baltimore Stars to two USFL championships, then moved on to the NFL to coach the New Orleans Saints and then the Indianapolis Colts. His son, Jim L. Mora, is currently the head football coach at UCLA.

Another candidate was Dick Coury, who was then the wide receivers coach for the Philadelphia Eagles. A third candidate was Rudy Hubbard, who was Florida A&M's head coach.

Fate was on my side. Jim, Dick and Rudy all dropped out!

When I got the job, I was ecstatic. Sure, building the Rainbow Warriors program was going to be an enormous challenge. But, as I mentioned before, I was ready. And I knew three very important things. I knew I had the ability to get players to play hard. I knew how to connect with players. And I knew I could really recruit.

The day after I was introduced as Hawaiʻi's new head coach, Bill Kwon of the *Honolulu Star-Bulletin* came out with a column headed, "New Hawaiʻi Coach a Positive Thinker."

Bill wrote, "If the Power of Positive Thinking can win football games, the University of Hawaiʻi has come up with a winner in its new coach, Dick Tomey (pronounced 'Tow-Mih')."

It wasn't until a couple of days after that column that Ray walked up to me and asked, "Do you want to discuss your salary?"

My salary hadn't even come up in our previous discussions. I didn't even ask. I just wanted the job.

"Sure," I responded. "What is it?"

I knew it wasn't going to be a lot of money. (My beginning salary was $30,000 plus another $5,000 for doing a coach's TV show.) But I figured that if I did a good job, I would eventually be compensated for it.

I felt on top of the world. I had achieved my goal of becoming a college football head coach, and I was going to get to live in the most beautiful place on Earth. I was also looking forward to working with so many Polynesian players. At UCLA, I had the opportunity to get to know players like Manu Tuiasosopo, Frank Manumaleuna and Mike Pavich (who played high school football for Punahou). They were all great family people with humble hearts.

"Dick Tomey, head coach, University of Hawaiʻi." That really had a nice ring to it.

Arriving at my office, I shut the door, walked to my desk and sat down. Finally, I had a moment to exhale. Locking my hands together, I twiddled my fingers and looked around.

Those two words again.

"What now?"

First item on the agenda: Take a vacation.

It's true. One of the first things I did after being hired was to take our family on a week-long vacation to Lake Tahoe. (Our son, Richie, was seven at the time. Our daughter, Angela, was three.) I know it sounds crazy, considering all the work that needed to be done. But I knew that the next few weeks and months were going to be impossibly hectic. This was our one chance to escape from the madness to come.

When we returned, I rolled up my sleeves and went to work. Fortunately, although building a winning football team was an imposing task, I knew I was going to have some quality help.

When a new head coach comes into a program, he usually gets to assemble his own staff. But my situation was different. Before I even accepted the job, I was told that six assistant coaches had recently signed one-year contracts with the school. Bringing in an entirely new staff was not an option.

Bob Wagner (UH assistant coach, 1977-82; defensive coordinator; head coach, 1987-95): *I was new to Hawai'i. I signed my contract in May and then went out to do some recruiting. Larry [Price] resigned a week or two later. The thing that was really interesting to me was that, when Ray was interviewing the new head coaching candidates, some of us assistant coaches got to go to lunch with them. I remember going to the Royal Hawaiian Hotel for the first time. We ate at the Surf Room right there by the beach. Jim Mora was one of the people being interviewed. I had been a grad assistant for him when he coached the defense at Washington. I also remember having lunch with Rudy Hubbard, who had played at Ohio State. Being a native of Newark, Ohio, I had a connection with Rudy as well.*

Everyone was excited when Dick was hired. There had been a lot of negativity going around, but here's a guy who left UCLA to become Hawai'i's head coach. Fortunately for me, Jim had coached with Dick for a brief time at UCLA, and he later called Dick on my behalf. I was actually in the middle of buying a home in Hawai'i Kai. I knew that I had a contract. Still, I asked Dick if he was open to keeping the existing staff around, or if he was going to bring in his own people. Dick just told me, "I want you to do such a good job that I'll have to retain you." That was good enough for me because I believed in myself. I bought the house.

After I got the UH job, I reached out to Larry Price. Larry was great. He was very supportive of me and wished me well. I tried not to be critical of Larry. You never want to come in and bash what your predecessor did. The fact is, the circumstances were better for me than they were for him.

I cannot say this enough: Larry Price did a fabulous job of putting together a staff. He brought in Bob Wagner from Washington, where he was a G.A. under head coach Don James. "Wags" was our defensive backs coach, and he was outstanding from the get-go. Ten years later, when I left Hawai'i in 1987, I don't think anyone was surprised when Bob took the reins of the program and led our team to the WAC championship and a victory in the Holiday Bowl.

Charlie Ka'aihue coached our defensive line. He was a two-time ILH all-star for Iolani and the legendary Father Kenneth A. Bray. The elder statesman of our staff (he was forty-four), Charlie was highly respected in local coaching circles. He was a high school All-American at Iolani and later played for the Philadelphia Eagles, Oakland Raiders and San Francisco 49ers.

Charlie played a really important role in helping me and some of the other coaches learn about Hawai'i. We were all hungry for knowledge about the state, the university and the team, and Charlie helped us bridge that divide. Just as importantly, our players loved Charlie, his wife, Marmie, and their daughter, Ulu. His younger brother, Henry, played for UH before becoming one of the great music icons in the Islands.

Henry Kapono Ka'aihue (UH defensive lineman, 1970): *When you looked at Charlie, you would think that he was pretty strict. And he was. But he also had a lot of compassion for his players. Everybody that played under him had a lot of respect for him.*

I remember that Charlie had a lot of respect for Coach Tomey. He did everything he could to make Coach Tomey and his family feel at home. He loved that family and would talk about them all the time.

Tom Tuinei (UH defensive lineman, 1976-79): *When I was being recruited, it came down to Washington and Hawai'i. Coach Ka'aihue was recruiting me. One day, after some really heavy rains, it was flooding in front of our yard, in our driveway and even along the main road. The water was two feet deep. Coach Ka'aihue came down to check up on us. He rolled up his pants and walked to my house to see me and my mom. That showed me that he cared about us. He cared about my family. That was a turning point in my decision to sign with Hawai'i.*

Another coach with local ties was George Lumpkin, who was in charge of our outside linebackers. George had been a terrific defensive back for Hawai'i—at one time he held the school career record for interceptions—and in 1971 he joined the coaching staff as a G.A. George is an African-American who lived most of his adult life in Hawai'i. In my mind, he was as "local" as they come. George, as seasoned Hawai'i fans know, would go on to have the longest UH coaching tenure of us all. He coached under, in order, Dave Holmes, Larry Price, myself, Bob Wagner, June Jones and Greg McMackin.

Rip Scherer was our running backs coach. Like Wags, Rip was new to the Islands, having been hired in February to tutor our quarterbacks. He had been a three-year quarterback for William & Mary, and later served as a part-time coach for Joe Paterno and the Penn State Nittany Lions. Rip was a tremendous offensive mind who would later become the offensive coordinator at Power Five schools such as Georgia Tech, Alabama and Arizona. He's still in the coaching ranks today as the tight ends coach for UCLA.

Having served on the coaching staff the two previous seasons, Tom Freeman was already one of the senior members of our brain trust. Tom was an All-Coast tackle at San Diego State before entering the coaching ranks. He later became a G.A. under the great Don Coryell before landing stints at Santa Ana College and San Diego City College. We put Tom in charge of our centers and guards.

Dan Dorazio, our tackles and tight ends coach, began his coaching career as a G.A. at his alma mater, Kent State. He had played both running back and receiver for the Golden Flashes. One of his teammates was Nick Saban, now the head coach of the Alabama Crimson Tide. A bit of history here: Dan enrolled at Kent State just weeks after the tragic May 4, 1970 massacre, when the Ohio National Guard opened fire on a group of students on campus, killing four and wounding nine others.

"I had already been accepted at Kent State," Dan later told the *Vancouver Sun*. "We didn't know if there'd be school. When we did get back to school, our first home game there were bomb threats. It was a changing time."

Like Bob Wagner, Dan served under Don James at Washington before joining the Rainbow Warriors staff.

I was able to add two of my own guys to our staff. I knew right away who I wanted to bring in, and both were willing to come to the program.

Bob Burt had been a G.A. at UCLA and a good friend of mine. His coaching work prior to serving on the Bruins staff included four very successful years at Santiago High School in Garden Grove, California, where he led the Cavaliers to four straight championships. We assigned Bob to lead our inside linebackers. And although he didn't carry the title of defensive coordinator, he basically oversaw our defensive scheme game planning.

Similarly, I brought in Mike Flores to organize our offense, although he was officially our quarterbacks and wide receivers coach. He was another G.A. and dear friend who served with me at UCLA (he played quarterback for the Bruins for one season). Although he was only twenty-five when he joined our staff, Mike had already been apprenticed by four NFL coaches, including Chuck Knox.

When Mike arrived in Honolulu, he made sure to bring his wry wit with him. "Dick, now that I'm here," he informed me with an easy grin, "the Hispanic population in Hawai'i just doubled."

In addition to our full-time staff, we had the services of part-time assistant John Wilbur. John had been an offensive lineman for the NFL's Dallas Cowboys, Los Angeles Rams and Washington Redskins. In fact, he was the starting right guard on the Redskins' Super Bowl VII team. In 1975, John played for The Hawaiians in the short-lived World Football League.

Mike Vasconcellos was a volunteer assistant with us. He and I had known each other for a while, and he was a great help. Mike would later become the longtime athletic director for Chaminade University. It was Mike who hired Merv Lopes as the school's head basketball coach, and we all know what happened after that: The Silverswords shocked No. 1-ranked Virginia in 1982, in what has got to be the greatest upset in college basketball history.

Also joining our staff was Rich Ellerson, who had just graduated from the University of Hawai'i. Rich had a solid playing career as a Rainbow Warrior, contributing as a hard-nosed linebacker before becoming our starting center in 1976. He joined my staff as an eager-to-learn G.A. He was resourceful, bright and had an undeniable work ethic—all qualities that would serve him well throughout his coaching career, both here at UH and later as head coach at three schools, including Army.

Rich Ellerson (UH LB/OL, 1974, 1975-76; assistant coach, 1977, 1981-83; defensive coordinator, 1987-91): *Being a G.A., you're the lowest guy on the totem pole. But it was my chance to dip my toes in the coaching waters, and I was anxious to learn and get to work. I was breaking down film, running the scout team and things like that. One thing I really remember was that we had a lot of broken headsets. So I would go up to our communications department and try to solder them back together. I did a horrible job!*

I do remember that my old teammates were pretty optimistic. Being from UCLA, Coach Tomey had a lot of credibility. For me, just having played at UH and still having friends on the team, my relationships [with the players] had to change a bit because now I had a foot in two different worlds. But it wasn't stressful or anything like that. You just have to be discreet in your conversations after you make that transition.

One of the funny things about Rich was that he was never afraid to speak his mind. In fact, he was the only guy on that first coaching staff who would argue with me. All the other guys wouldn't challenge me because they were petrified they might get fired. Not Rich. Rich would debate anything at the drop of a hat, whether it was football strategy or politics or philosophy or whatever.

Rich Ellerson: *Coach says that all the time! (Laughs.) And my response is, Well, yeah. Whenever Coach asked a question, I just assumed that he wanted to hear what I thought. I don't remember in any way being argumentative, but I wasn't shy about offering opinions. I thought Coach Tomey was looking for some help because he had basically just walked into our program, and I felt it was incumbent upon those of us who'd been around the block a little to put things in context. I mean, if you ask, I'll tell you what I think.*

We had a quality coaching staff. Four of our assistant coaches from this 1977 UH team would go on to become college football head coaches: Bob Burt (Cal State Northridge); Rich Ellerson (Southern Utah, Cal Poly and Army); Rip Scherer (James Madison and Memphis); and Bob Wagner (Hawai'i).

When our staff got together for the first time, I told them that I wasn't going to do what some other coaches might do in this situation. I had no intention of firing them at the end of the season so that I could bring in more of my own coaches.

"I'm going to try to help us all work together in such a way that we'll want to coach together for a long time," I said.

I also told them, "There is somebody that I want to bring in for next season, and if somebody leaves, he will replace that person. If nobody leaves, we'll have to make a tough decision. We'll wait and see what happens."

The coach I wanted to bring in was Ed Kezirian, who was at UCLA at the time. I felt it was important to be up front with my staff about my intentions. And as it turned out, Ed did join us for the 1978 season. And I did have to make a tough decision.

The coach I wound up letting go after our first season was Dan Dorazio. Dan was a great guy, and I told our staff, "This doesn't mean that Dan is the lesser of anybody here. He will be able to get another job immediately."

I was right. It didn't take long for Dan to find work. He joined the coaching staff at San Jose State and, later, the University of Washington. After leaving the college ranks, he became an offensive line coach in the Canadian Football League for more than forty years. In fact, Dan is still at it. He's now with the league's BC Lions.

The first big priority for our staff was recruiting, but not in the way that you might expect. Instead of looking to bring in new players, our chief goal was to "re-recruit" the players who were already on our roster. I always felt that, when you get a head coaching job, so many times you don't spend enough time with the team you have. We knew we could find new players, but it was so much more important to spend time with the players we already had. We wanted them to get to know us and give them something to feel good about. Had we not done that, I don't think our program would have had the success that we eventually had.

And that brings me back to Blane Gaison.

Blane was one of our returning quarterbacks. He'd seen some action the previous season as a true freshman out of Kamehameha-Kapālama, finishing as the team's second-leading passer with 168 passing yards and a touchdown. (Larry Price's teams ran the "Hula T" offense, which was primarily focused on running the ball.

For whatever reason, Blane was not happy in the program and was looking to transfer to Boise State. Knowledgeable people within and outside the university told me that I should meet with Blane and try to convince him to stay.

Blane Gaison (UH DB/QB, 1976-80): *Things just didn't go well (the previous season). It didn't meet the expectations that I had. And so at the end of the 1976 season, I decided that I was going to leave. Because of the NCAA rules back then, I had to finish the school year first in order to transfer to another school.*

During this process, Larry Price resigned. Ray Nagel gave me a call and told me that they were looking for a new coach, and that he wanted me to reconsider my decision. Ray asked me if I would be willing to sit down and meet with the new head coach.

I was just a young kid, not thinking straight, and just wanting to leave. When they hired Coach Tomey, I didn't know him from Adam. But Coach called me from L.A. and said he wanted to meet with me and my parents. I thought, "Really? Why would you want to meet with me?"

Several days later, he was here at my house in Kāneʻohe. He sat down with us and laid out his plan for the University of Hawaiʻi. He talked about what he had done and what he hoped to do here. He was very straightforward with us, very genuine and forthright. He said, "I'm not going to make any promises to you. I don't know you very well, but I've heard a lot about you. I can tell you one thing: If you decide to stay at the University of Hawaiʻi, you will not be disappointed." Then he left. He was at the house for maybe an hour and fifteen minutes.

My Dad was a military guy, and so I grew up in a household where discipline was very important. I thought he was a very good judge of character. Well, Dad looked at me and said, "I like that guy. He laid out his plan and threw everything on the table. You asked him questions and he gave you straight answers."

After that, I just unpacked my bags. Coach Tomey left such an impression on me that I figured that the right thing for me to do was to unpack my bags and stay home.

Jack Wright was one of our returning offensive lineman. He joined the program out of Punahou as a walk-on in 1975, and eventually, through hard work, earned a spot in the starting lineup. Jack played in the very first game at Aloha Stadium, when Hawaiʻi hosted Texas A&I on September 13, 1975. Texas A&I is now known as Texas A&M-Kingsville, a Division II institution with a proud football legacy. Three of their alumni are in the Pro Football Hall of Fame: Gene Upshaw, Darrell Green and John Randle.

Jack Wright (UH OL, 1975-78): *I met Coach Tomey after he got hired. I happened to be in California at the time. I was staying with my [Punahou] classmate and best friend, Mosi Tatupu. So Coach calls me and introduces himself.*

"Hi, Jack. I'm Dick Tomey, the new head coach at the University of Hawaiʻi."

"Hi, Coach. Nice to meet you. How did you get my number?"

"I called your Mom. Do you have some time to meet with me today?"

I informed him that I was on the Mainland, and Coach said, "Me, too. I'm over at UCLA right now."

So I head over to UCLA and to see him. Now, I was about six feet tall and about 220 pounds. I wasn't a huge lineman by any stretch. I walk in, and he just looked at me. I'm sure he was thinking, "You've got to be kidding me. This is my starting offensive guard?"

One of the first things he said to me was, "No one's got a guaranteed starting job," which was fine with me. I wanted to earn my position like everybody else. And everything worked out great.

Another returning player was wide receiver DeWayne Jett. (What a perfect name for a receiver!) DeWayne showed some real promise as a freshman in 1976, with seven receptions for 137 yards. He also led the team in kickoff return yards. He was another guy who was thinking about leaving the program, but a chance encounter allowed me to convince him to stay.

DeWayne Jett (UH WR, 1976-79): *Let me tell you how I first met Coach Tomey. I actually met him before he even got to the University of Hawai'i. I played my freshman season for UH in 1976. By the end of that school year, I already had three individual position coaches. Then, I headed back to Los Angeles to see my family, and I find out that Larry Price was no longer with the program. People were saying that the program was unstable, and I heard a lot of players talking about leaving. I was a little discouraged, so I decided to test the waters.*

UCLA was interested in me before I chose to attend UH, so I wanted to see if the Bruins might want to re-recruit me. I went over to talk to [Bruins head coach] Terry Donahue. I let them know what I had done as a freshman at Hawai'i. There was another guy in the office as I was speaking to Coach Donahue. Coach gave me some advice, and I thanked him and started to walk out. The other guy asked me, "I'm going to lunch. Can I talk to you for a little while?"

That guy was Dick Tomey. He was still on the UCLA staff at the time, and he had just accepted the Hawai'i job. He said, "I'm going to become the head coach at the University of Hawai'i, and I'd really appreciate it if you stay. That's how we met! (Laughs.) Not many people know this story.

Jeff Duva, who wound up being our starting quarterback during my first two seasons in Hawai'i, was a transfer from San Diego State via BYU. Larry Price had brought him in to compete for the starting position with Blane and Bob Acosta.

Jeff Duva (UH QB, 1977-78): *At the time, Hawai'i was not in a conference, and it was the only Division I school that you could transfer to and play immediately. I knew almost nothing about the UH program, although I do remember role-playing "Alex Kaloi" on the BYU scout team when I was a freshman in 1974, when Alex was the Hawai'i quarterback.*

Right before I scheduled my trip to Hawai'i, Coach Price resigned. So I just waited for the new head coach to be announced. I made my trip to the Islands at the same time Coach Tomey took the job. We had dinner at the Hyatt Regency Hotel in Waikīkī. It was an exciting time for me, being in a new place and having a fresh start.

Coach Tomey was fantastic. He was very positive and had a lot of energy. He had a lot of big goals that he had for us to achieve, and that's exactly what I was looking for. I didn't want to be in a program that was in the doldrums. I wanted to be in a program that was on the rise and on the move. I wanted to be on a team that could do some great things, and that's what I felt from Coach. He was going to bring that attitude and atmosphere to Hawai'i football.

Our starting defensive tackle, Harris Matsushima, gave us no indication that he wanted to transfer from the program, but I made sure to visit him and his family, anyway. They could not have been more respectful. At 6-2, 245 pounds, Harris was a terrific lineman and one of the leaders on our team.

There were other returnees that I felt I could count on, guys like defensive linemen Tom Tuinei and Gary Spotts, receiver Jeff Cabral, placekicker Curtis Goodman, tight end Jerry Scanlan, and defensive backs Keoni Jardine and Bryan Hanawahine.

Fullback Wilbert Haslip was the team's leading returning offensive player. I had admired Wil back when he was at Santa Ana Valley High School in California. Tom Baldwin, the coach at Santa Ana, was a good friend of mine. From all accounts, Wil was an outstanding young man, and he wound up doing a really good job for us.

Because we were not yet in the Western Athletic Conference—or any conference—players from other schools could transfer to Hawai'i and be eligible to play immediately. We did our best to take full advantage of that.

Pat Schmidt was a big "get" for our program. Pat was a two-year starter at UCLA who could hit you like a ton of bricks. It was Pat's fourth-quarter interception of Cornelius Green that sealed the Bruins' win over previously undefeated and No. 1-ranked Ohio State in the 1976 Rose Bowl. But UCLA was bringing in a future Pro Football Hall of Famer in Kenny Easley, and Pat was looking for a change of scenery.

Pat Schmidt (UH FS, 1977): *I had gotten into a bit of trouble in Los Angeles. When Coach Tomey announced that he was leaving UCLA to take over the Hawai'i program, he came up to me and said, "Maybe you can use a change of scenery. Would you like to go to Hawai'i with me?" And I said, "Let me think about it for a minute. Yes, I would!"*

I felt like I was the team's senior citizen. I knew Coach Tomey, and I knew the system he ran. I think he leaned on me and other UCLA transfers like Tom Clark and Tom Murphy to lead by example.

When we first got the team together, I explained that time was not on our side. We just had a few weeks to prepare for our season-opening game against the New Mexico Lobos. As a result, we were going to keep things very simple.

"Football is not complicated," I said. "People are."

It's true, and it's still central to what I believe. We could not afford to overcomplicate things, particularly when we had just gotten together and were already looking down the barrel of the season.

I also told the team something that I think surprised them: The most important thing we needed to do was not about football. Instead, it was about getting to know each other.

Remember, this was a unique situation we were in. The coaches didn't know the players. The players didn't know the coaches. Heck, most of our coaches were just getting to know each other, and the same could be said of our players. It was so important for us to learn about each other and be invested in staying together.

That first night, we gathered in the dining room of one of the dormitories. All the coaches tried to meet as many of the players as we could. Everyone was excited.

Blane Gaison: *Right away, we could tell that Coach Tomey was a man with a very special spirit. He told us what we could expect of him and what he expected of us. He spoke straight to the heart of every person in the room. Coach made us believe—we bought in—and we couldn't wait for the next morning to have our first practice!*

Looking back on that first meeting, I regret that I failed to meet with each player individually. I think it was important for me as the head coach to do that. I should have said, "I want to meet with you guys one on one and have a ten-minute conversation with each and every one of you. We can do this for the rest of the night and, if need be, start again in the morning."

It was a mistake that I made sure to correct in future years.

Jeff Duva: *When we started two-a-days in early August, Coach Tomey had everyone take a piece of white ankle tape, write our names on it and then stick it to the front of our helmets. That was something I hadn't done since my Pee Wee or Pop Warner days. It sounds crazy because it was just weeks before the start of the season, and our first task was to learn everyone's names.*

Coach Tomey had a real knack for team building and bonding. He would have players come over to his house to relax and have a steak dinner with his family. He would also do things like cut practice short to have an offense versus defense swimming competition at the swimming pool or a slip-and-slide competition on our practice field.

Eventually, we became a close unit. We were so tight and bonded together. Everybody was pulling the next guy up if he was down. It was almost like the movie The Longest Yard, *where you had all these guys that came together from different walks of life and different universities. We just bonded into a family.*

Bryan Hanawahine (UH DB, 1975-78): *In camp, at every meal we had to sit with somebody different. Coach didn't want to see you sitting with the same people. He made us mingle with one another to break down any barriers between the local players and Mainland players. We still had our walls up a bit, but as we got to know each other we all got along well. We got to learn each other's cultures and lifestyles. In later years, when I got the opportunity to coach, I tried to do the same thing with our student-athletes.*

Blane Gaison: *Coach Tomey really didn't have a lot of time to get things together. He didn't have spring practice with us. It was just a unique situation. He came in and called a meeting when we first started to report. It was amazing. Here was this haole guy coming in and talking about family and love. He said the first thing that we needed to do was learn to love one another.*

There we were, a bunch of eighteen-, nineteen- and twenty-year-old guys that are out there to play football, and here's this coach coming in and talking about loving one another! But you know what? It hit home for a lot of us, especially the kids from Hawaiʻi because that was our culture. The local culture was about family, ʻohana and love. It's about caring for one another.

We did everything we could to promote unity. At team picnics and other social gatherings, we played Cecilio & Kapono's *Friends* over and over and over. I'm sure more than a few players might have gotten sick of hearing the song, but the message was exactly what we wanted to convey: *We are friends.*

Our emphasis on unity wasn't just for this first season. It was something we continually preached at UH, and then later on at Arizona and San Jose State. One year, the UH dorms weren't available, and we had no place for the players to stay. But rather than getting bent out of shape about it, we made the best of the situation by turning the practice gym into a makeshift dormitory. We laid down four mattresses in one area and called it "Room 1-A," then added four more mattresses in another area and called it "Room 1-B," and so on. All of our guys were assigned to different areas.

When the players checked in that day, we had a big sign up that read, "RAINBOW HILTON." We just had fun with it!

There were a hundred players and about a dozen coaches in there. It was great because all the guys really had to be unselfish in terms of the noise that they made. Once it was bedtime, everyone had to be quiet so that no one's sleep would be disturbed.

To this day, the "Rainbow Hilton" is a very fond memory for me. We had turned a negative into a positive.

My methods to build team chemistry and enhance our team concept were nowhere near as developed as they became in the mid-1980s, when I met the renowned master motivator and life strategist Tony Robbins. We'll get to Tony in a later chapter.

To underscore the importance of getting to know our players, I had this rule for our entire coaching staff: "If a player comes in here and wants to talk to me, I'm going to talk to him rather than talk to you. And if he comes by to see you, you will talk to him rather than talk to me. If a player comes all way in here to see us, it must be important to him. Excuse yourself from whatever you're doing and talk to him."

Carol Pangan was our secretary, and she was fabulous. I told her the very same thing: "If we're having a coaches meeting and one of the players stops by to see any one of us, interrupt us. Nothing's more important than they are."

I also told the coaches that the worst place to talk to somebody is your office. For a lot of young people, it's like being in the principal's office. You want the player to be relaxed. I suggested to our coaches that they take their players out for a walk around the campus. That's a far better way to get a discussion going.

As I mentioned earlier, we were pressed for time in preparing for our first game of the season. Simplicity would be key. I think the players expected us to just immerse themselves in football, but nothing could be further from the truth.

We would not have a complicated playbook. That first year, we only had five running plays and six passing plays, along with some situational stuff and special plays. On defense, we had one defensive front early in the season and several coverage packages. We had maybe one scheme for our special teams unit. To try to implement a complex playbook when we've only been together for a few weeks was, in my mind, ridiculous.

I remember one day that summer when our offensive and defensive staffs were meeting separately in one of our Quonset huts on the lower campus. I could hear our offensive coaches talking back and forth. Rip Scherer and Mike Flores were organizing our offense. I passed by one of them on the way to the restroom and asked, "How's the meeting going?"

The response floored me. "Well, we're in the middle of a discussion on how we're going to huddle."

I just lost it. They had spent an hour and a half discussing how they wanted the offense to huddle!

I stormed into the room and said, "You know how we're going to huddle? The first time we get the offense together, we're going to say, 'Huddle up!' And whatever they do, that's the way we're going to huddle. Discussion over."

The idea was, rather than bury ourselves with schematics, we were going to run a few plays and run them right. We were going to be unselfish and pull for each other.

And we were going to play our asses off.

We also put a focus on not getting penalized a great deal. Players from Hawaiʻi had a reputation of being heavily penalized because they liked to be viewed as ferocious hitters. They loved to hit. It was our job to find a way to make them understand that avoiding penalties required another kind of toughness. Winning had to be more important to you than making a great but illegal hit just to get a crowd reaction.

We also found ways to instill discipline in our program. We started "Dawn Patrol," where if you missed a class or broke another team rule you had to get up early in the morning—usually at five o'clock—and run with me. The rule was, if you were ahead of me at the end of two miles, you were done. If I was ahead, keep running. Now, I was an avid runner, even running a marathon. Hardly any of the guys got ahead of me.

The days flew by. Before we knew it, the 1977 season was upon us.

It was time to huddle up for real.

Chapter Three

THE FIRST SEASON

In football, some things never change. After every fall camp, by the time you get to the first game on the schedule, you're so sick and tired of hitting each other. You're just chomping at the bit to hit somebody you don't know. That's true for every school and for every season opener.

Heading into our first game against New Mexico, our Hawai'i fan base wasn't sure what to expect. There were so many unknowns, so many questions. What was our offense going to be like? How about the defense? Can this Dick Tomey guy coach? Could we even be competitive?

There were still doubters. During the summer and fall, I made as many public appearances as I could at various events, from Elks Club meetings to booster club gatherings and everything in between. Everywhere I went, I encountered some degree of negativity and skepticism. It reached a point where I instructed my coaches to simply ignore the cynics. We should always be courteous and respectful to everyone, I told them, but we need to push the negative stuff aside. It seemed everybody had their reasons for why we could not succeed. I wasn't interested in any of that. I was focused on how we could succeed.

Saturday, September 10. Hawai'i versus New Mexico at Aloha Stadium.

It was time for us to show the football world what we could do.

People ask me if I was able to sleep the night before the game. After all, it was my big head coaching debut on the college football Division I level. I'm sure I had a few butterflies in my stomach. But the truth is I was more focused on making sure we had every detail covered as kickoff approached. I was too busy to be nervous.

I had already taken care of one important matter. Before the game, UH Marching Band director Richard Lum called me and asked, "Coach, what do you want us to play when you guys come out on the field?"

I pondered the question for a moment. Then I remembered that I had met the great actor, Jack Lord, the day before.

"Hawai'i Five-0," I answered. It stuck.

New Mexico posed a big challenge for us. They had an outstanding running back in 6-2, 190-pound Mike Williams, who would later play three seasons for the Kansas City Chiefs. He would be one of the best backs we'd face all season. The Lobos' head coach was Bill Mondt, who was entering his fourth season with the program. The bookmakers had the Lobos favored by two touchdowns.

I had heard that Hawai'i fans were a late-arriving crowd. The games would start, and half the folks would still be tailgating in the parking lot. So we wanted to do something to get the fans' attention right away.

On our very first play from scrimmage, we ran a reverse flea-flicker. We had Jeff Duva under center as our quarterback. Blane Gaison was lined up at flanker. At the snap, Jeff pitched the ball to tailback Gerald Green, who in turn handed the ball to Blane on a reverse. Blane looked downfield and connected on a 30-yard pass to Jeff Cabral.

Welcome to Rainbow Warrior football!

The 26,532 fans in attendance cheered wildly. We had, indeed, gotten their attention.

We scored on that first possession, with Curtis Goodman booting a field goal from 38 yards out. Then the Lobos came at us hard.

Quarterback Noel Mazzone scored on a 50-yard scamper. Then Williams scored on a short run. That was followed by a fumble return for another score, and then Mazzone threw for a touchdown. Just like that, we were down 27-3 at halftime.

It was a disappointing way to open the season, and I lashed into our team pretty good in our locker room. If the game ended at the half, I would have been very discouraged.

But then came the second half.

Jeff moved us down the field at the start of the third quarter, using his running ability for a pair of first downs. Gerald Green scored from one yard out to make the score 27-10. Gerald, a speedy tailback from Purcell, Oklahoma, really emerged as an offensive threat for us in this game, finishing with 124 yards rushing on 22 carries.

In the fourth quarter, Jeff got on a roll, completing passes to Gerald, Rick Wagner and Jerry Scanlan. On second-and-one from the one-yard line, Wilbert Haslip tried to bull his way over the goal line, but the ball popped out from his grip. Lobos free safety Max Hudspeth scooped up the ball and raced to the opposite end zone.

Game over? Not quite. There was a flag on the field. New Mexico was called for offsides.

On the next play, Jeff snuck into the end zone for the score, then followed up with a two-point conversion to flanker Walt Little. On New Mexico's next possession, linebacker Joe Panora recovered a fumble for us on our 35-yard line.

Bobby Acosta came into the game for Jeff and led our offense 63 yards down the field. George Bell, a freshman tailback who joined our program from El Centro, California, powered in for the score. Suddenly, the score was 35-26.

And that was the score when the final gun sounded.

Coach Mondt was very generous in his appraisal of our team. "I think Hawai'i could be the fastest improving team in the country," he told the *Honolulu Star-Bulletin*'s Rod Ohira after the game. "It's a credit to Dick Tomey when you consider his team can play like that after only three weeks together."

The result was disappointing, but I still came away feeling encouraged. We could have folded after the first half, but we collected ourselves and made the game competitive. Most of all, we now had game film that we could take back and study. As a coach, it's vital that you get your team to invest in personal development and improvement. With this game under our belts, we could now evaluate our performance and see what we needed to do to get better. It was an opportunity for us to grow and take a step forward.

Unfortunately, besides losing the contest, we also wound up losing Blane. He tore some ligaments in his right knee during the game. He would sit out the rest of the year as a redshirt.

> **Blane Gaison:** *Coming out of training camp, Jeff Duva and I were going head-to-head for the starting quarterback position. The week of the New Mexico game, Coach Tomey and Coach Flores had basically decided that Jeff would start the first quarter, and then I would come in and play the second quarter. Whoever had the edge and was moving the ball would start the second half. Unfortunately, that never happened because I got hurt. Looking back on it, however, it was a blessing in disguise.*
>
> *It was definitely an exciting game. The stands were packed and the fans were really excited. That was the beginning of a tremendous run.*

Our Week Two opponent, Colorado State, had had a more successful season debut, pounding the University of the Pacific, 20-3, in Stockton, California. Their coach, Sark Arslanian, was in his fifth season with the Rams. Before that, he led the Weber State program for eight seasons and became the school's all-time winningest coach.

Like the New Mexico game, our game against CSU was a knock-down, drag-out battle. We got the edge midway through the first quarter when Burton Coloma, a sophomore cornerback out of Waialua High School, recovered a Rams fumble at their 15-yard line. A couple of plays later, Wilbert Haslip burst untouched into the end zone for the game's first score.

Curtis Goodman followed Wil's touchdown with two field goals. We were up 13-0 at the half.

Our defense in that first stanza was firing on all cylinders. Our defensive line, led by Harris Matsushima and Gary Spotts, was wreaking havoc in the trenches. Pat Schmidt was laying the wood on Rams receivers and backs. Our punter, Greg Cummins, wowed the home fans by averaging 44 yards on eight punts. But the biggest contributor on this night was Burton, who was a late addition to the team after transferring from Snow College in Utah. Burton had two fumble recoveries in the game.

In the end, however, the Rams rallied in the second half to win the game, 20-16, sending the 26,193 fans at Aloha Stadium home disappointed. There was no shame in losing to CSU, who would finish their season 9-2-1. We simply lacked the poise to get the job done when it mattered.

There was an interesting side note to the CSU game. The head coach at Snow College was Dave Arslanian, Sark's son. Just a few weeks earlier, Sark had seen Burton in a Snow College Badgers uniform, and he did a double take when he now saw Burton wearing Rainbow Warriors green and white!

Our next opponent, the Idaho Vandals, arrived in Honolulu looking for a win. Like us, the Vandals were 0-2 to start the season.

We went with a no-huddle offense to start the game. The first unit sprinted onto the field and ran a series of no-huddle plays. Then we pulled the first-string guys and put in the second unit. Again, no huddle. Our second unit guys ran straight to the line of scrimmage and snapped the ball. We steadily moved down the field, and then the first unit entered the game again.

We had the Idaho defense on their heels. They had no way of knowing we were going to start the game like this. And our fans were going absolutely nuts! They were on their feet and loving every second of what was happening.

The next play we had scripted was a 40-yard pass. The problem was, our offense was already positioned at the Vandals' seven-yard line. We needed a short-yardage play, not a 40-yard pass. Jeff Duva had the plays written on his wristband. He looked at the play, threw up his hands and called a time out.

It seemed like all 25,463 fans in attendance gave a collective groan. Our no-huddle trickery had finally stalled. To make matters worse, Curtis' field goal attempt went wide left.

Idaho put up the first points of the game, making good on a field goal late in the first quarter. Early in the second period, however, Pat Schmidt picked off a pass deep in our territory to prevent another Vandals score. Then Jeff led our offense on a lengthy drive that resulted in a 39-yard field goal.

Wilbert Haslip and his backup, Keith Hill, each scored touchdowns before intermission. We led 17-6 as both teams headed to their locker rooms. We were playing well, but we couldn't get comfortable. Remember, we had led Colorado State at halftime, too.

As it turned out, my concern was unfounded. We dominated the second half.

Everyone contributed in this game. Pat finished the game with two interceptions and a fumble recovery. Jeff did a good job spreading the ball around, firing passes to Gerald Green, Jeff Cabral and Jerry Scanlan. Keoni Jardine came up with a big interception to prevent an Idaho touchdown. George Bell ran in from five yards for a touchdown. Mike Stennis, our sophomore backup at quarterback, raced 21 yards for a score. Even freshman kicker Stan Kua got in on the action, booting an extra point to seal our 45-26 victory.

One of the night's biggest plays was a 54-yard touchdown strike from Jeff to DeWayne Jett.

> **DeWayne Jett:** *I'll tell you why I remember that touchdown. Their defensive back was talking smack, as defensive backs usually do. I was never that talkative during the games. I usually let my play do my talking. But I remember catching that pass from Jeff. I stretched and dove for the ball, and the DB landed on me. He was trying to show that he had me covered, I guess. Anyway, I scored the touchdown and turned to the crowd to celebrate. Jerry Scanlan was the first to reach me and pick me up. The Idaho DB walked up from behind me and tried to knock the ball out of my hand. I threw the ball at him, and the referees threw a flag.*
>
> *Everyone was cheering me and showering me with accolades as I walked back to the bench. But Coach Tomey grabbed me by my jersey and said to me, "You're not worth fifteen yards!"*
>
> *It was the only unsportsmanlike penalty I ever had in my playing career, from Pop Warner through the pros.*

Although the Idaho game was a complete team victory, one Rainbow Warrior stood out in particular. Basically, this was Wilbert Haslip's coming out party. Wil powered his way to 221 rushing yards on 22 carries. He eclipsed Larry Sherrer's UH single-game record for rushing yards (Larry had run for 196 yards against Santa Clara in 1971) and became the first Hawai'i back to break the 200-yard mark in a game.

Credit should also be given to our offensive line, who created the holes for Wil to burst through. Guys like Tom Clark, Greg McElroy, Jack Wright, Kevin Scullion, Chris Johnston, Beldon Kealoha and Stan Quina all contributed to our strong ground attack.

For his efforts, Wil was named to UPI's Backfield of the Week, sharing the honor with BYU quarterback Gifford Nielson, Iowa State running back Dexter Green and Pittsburgh fullback Elliot Walker. Everyone on the team was happy for Wil, a great young man who was developing into one of the leaders on our offense.

It was my first victory as a Division I college football head coach. I didn't get to enjoy it for very long, however. Southwestern Louisiana was coming to town, and they were a terrific team.

The Ragin' Cajuns, in fact, arrived in Honolulu with a spotless 4-0 record, having beaten Tulsa, Fresno State, Lamar and Texas Arlington. They had some really good players, including quarterback Roy Henry and a freshman tight end

Tight end Ron Hall makes a reception against BYU.

Top: The Rainbow Warriors gave national contender USC a scare in 1978. **Above:** Gary Allen carries the ball against Colorado State.

Top: In 1977 defensive back Burton Coloma blocks a punt in a big win over South Carolina.
Above: The '77 Rainbow Warriors, the team that started it all..

Top: Blane Gaison starts his first game of the season at quarterback after playing as starting safety, and leads the Rainbow Warriors to victory against Pac-10 power Arizona State. Above: Fans pack the Aloha Stadium parking lot for pre-game tailgate parties in 1980.

Top: With the Rainbow Warriors trailing 7-5 in the fourth quarter, quarterback Jeff Duva takes a snap against USC. Above: Linebacker Anthony Woodson makes like Superman against Utah in 1981.

Top: Duane Coleman, Bernard Carvalho, Dino Babers, Mark Gardner and Nick Castro take their Senior Walk in 1983. **Above:** Dick Tomey accepts the Kuter Trophy after a win over Air Force in 1980.

Top: Running back David Toloumu carries the ball against USC. **Above:** Ti leaves are a fan staple at Aloha Stadium, here in 1981.

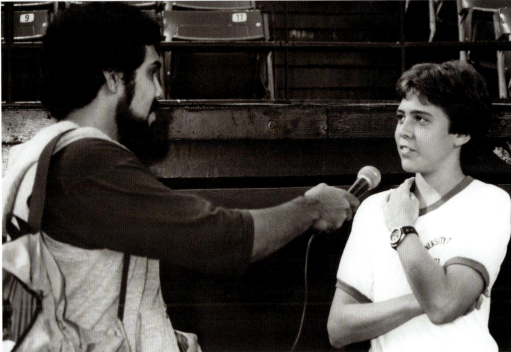

Top: The defense celebrates a late fumble, caused by Doug Kyle and recovered by Mark Kafentzis, to key the 1980 upset of West Virginia. **Above:** Rich Tomey gives an interview on the art of holding his father's headset cord during the games.

named Calvin James.

The game represented our biggest challenge to date, and our fans sensed it. More than 30,000 fans—31,762, to be exact—filed into Aloha Stadium in anticipation of a hard-fought contest. No one left disappointed.

We again used some sleight-of-hand to gain an advantage. Late in the second quarter, Jeff Duva shoveled the ball to our reserve fullback, Keith Hill. Keith, a junior from Chicago, rolled to his left and lofted a perfect pass to receiver Rick Wagner for the score. The touchdown gave us both the momentum and a 14-6 lead going into halftime. As it turned out, that was all the scoring we needed. Curtis Goodman kicked a pair of field goals in the second half, and our defense shut out SLU the rest of the way. We won the game, 20-6.

We again displayed a dominant running attack, putting up 251 yards rushing against the Ragin' Cajuns. This time around, it was freshman tailback George Bell who shined, gaining 132 yards on 22 rushing attempts. Our offensive line did a stellar job throughout the game, protecting Jeff (11-for-17 for 128 yards passing) and opening holes for our backs.

Jack Wright: *I really have to credit our coaches. They tailored a scheme for us that was very simple but also made very good use of the personnel that we had. We had basic plays with different options and misdirections. I wasn't a huge guy, but I could run. I could trap and pull. The coaches gave us simple schemes that we were able to grasp fairly quickly.*

Tom Freeman was a great offensive line coach. He broke everything down for us and was an excellent technician and strategist. With Coach Freeman, we learned how to change a blocking scheme at the line of scrimmage in two seconds. We were always well prepared.

A few days after defeating SLU, we flew to Stockton, California for our first road game of the season—an October 8 contest against Pacific. At this point, we had won two straight games and were feeling pretty good about ourselves.

You can guess what happened next. We got embarrassed, 37-7.

It was a wake-up call for us. We got beat physically and mentally. We had no excuses. We were just caught with our pants down.

"We were out-coached, out-played and out-fought," I told *The Honolulu Advertiser* after the game. "We were so dominated, if we had any ideas about being a good football team, we'll have to reevaluate."

Our lone score of the contest came near the end of the first quarter, with Jeff throwing a 13-yard touchdown pass to junior tight end Mike Jackson. That put us in front, 7-3. The Tigers just dominated the rest of the way, scoring 34 straight points.

It was a dismal effort all the way around. Our usually sure-handed offense fumbled five times, losing four of them. We put in Bobby Acosta to relieve Jeff at quarterback, and his first pass was an interception.

I didn't do a good job of preparing our team for either the game or the road experience. Charlie Kaʻaihue and some of the other coaches tried to help me, but I clearly didn't do a good job getting our players ready for this game. I should have made the guys aware that Pacific was probably going to be the best team we'd played up until that point.

The good news is, in time we learned to become a really good road team. I don't think you're at a disadvantage when you're on the road unless you think you are. When you go on the road with a negative attitude, you start preparing differently and getting distracted. In our case, we also had a bunch of players who were from California and were excited about seeing their family and friends. We weren't as focused as we needed to be.

There is one side note to this game. Our road trip showed me just how important SPAM was to all the kids from Hawaiʻi. In Stockton, all the guys loaded up on SPAM. When we got back to Honolulu and went to the baggage claim area, I can't begin to tell you how many cases of SPAM there were coming around the carousel!

Again, we didn't have a lot of time to lick our wounds. We had a game against Southern Mississippi the next Saturday at Aloha Stadium.

In those days, exchanging game film was an accepted practice in college football. When Alabama played Auburn, for example, coaches from both schools would drive to some midway point between Tuscaloosa and Auburn to exchange game film. Back then, there was no video. You had to physically cut up the film and splice everything together with a little machine. Sometimes you'd be running a film and everything would be upside down.

Today, of course, teams are able to scout their opponents with ease. Games are all over the Internet, and you can receive separate videos for offense, defense and special teams. But in 1977, none of that technology was yet available. Coaching staffs then were mired in the Dark Ages.

Why am I telling you this? Well, we had sent our game film to Southern Mississippi via air mail, as usual. But we kept waiting for the Golden Eagles' film to arrive. As our game drew closer, I called their head coach, Bobby Collins.

"Coach, where's our tape?" I asked.

Bobby was embarrassed. "Aw, Coach," he replied, "we sent it via general mail."

The Southern Miss coaches sent their game film to us via boat. We eventually got the package three weeks after the game.

How much of a difference did it make? There's no way of really knowing. I can tell you that it was a close, hard-fought contest that wasn't decided until the final twelve seconds.

We put up the game's first points. After linebacker Tom Murphy recovered a fumble on the Golden Eagles' first possession, Curtis Goodman placed a 22-yard kick through the uprights, giving us a 3-0 lead. Tom had a terrific game for us, with 13 tackles to go along with his fumble recovery. Other defensive standouts for the home team included lineman Tom Tuinei and linebacker Mike Arvanetis, each of whom had 14 tackles, as well as tackle Fialele Edra, who had two fumble recoveries.

Late in the first quarter, trailing 7-3, Jeff completed a pass to Mike Jackson, who broke a tackle attempt and sprinted down the *mauka* sideline for a 43-yard score. The lone score in the second quarter was another Curtis Goodman field goal, this time from 40 yards out.

Southern Miss struck for three touchdowns in the third quarter, including an 80-yard strike from their sophomore quarterback, Dane McDaniel.

It all came down to the final possession of the game. Trailing 28-26, we had one more chance to pull off a win. Jeff completed a 26-yard pass to Walt Little, who was downed at the Southern Miss 30. Gerald Green ran for three yards, then raced around the right end for another 9-yard gain. Wil Haslip plowed through the middle of the line to the Southern Miss 10-yard line. With twelve seconds left, we sent Curtis into the game.

I will never forget what happened next. We lined up for the field goal. The home crowd of 26,474 was buzzing with anticipation. Jeff, who was our placeholder, took the snap and placed the ball down. Curtis charged the ball, winding up for the game-winning kick.

And then, *THUD*.

Jeff didn't get his hand out of the way in time, and the ball just sort of dribbled off the tee. Game over.

It was just a bizarre play. I had never seen that happen before. I felt bad for Jeff, who had a big welt on his hand afterward. No one wanted to win the game more than he did.

The 1977 Rainbow Warriors were now 2-4 on the season with five games left to play.

Our next opponent was Portland State. Their head coach was Darrell "Mouse" Davis, who is widely regarded as the Godfather of the run and shoot offense that served Hawai'i so well during June Jones' time as UH head coach. It was Mouse that introduced June to the run and shoot. June, who played at UH before transferring to Portland State, set numerous records as the Vikings' quarterback in 1975 and 1976.

Portland State arrived in Honolulu sporting a 3-3 record. The Vikings were a Division I-AA school (now known as Football Championship Subdivision, or FCS), but we were not about to take them lightly. Their offense was averaging more than 32 points a game.

Unfortunately, we came out flat in the first half. I later told the media that it was our worst half of the season in terms of intensity. We were flagged for too many penalties and could not capitalize on our opportunities. A 5-yard rushing touchdown by George Bell put us in front at halftime, 7-6.

It was our defense that came through for us on this night. We had five big interceptions, including one in the end zone that defensive back Vaness Harris ran back to the Vikings' 49-yard-line. Pat Schmidt, Bryan Hanawahine, Tom Knight and Mike Otto also picked off passes. Mouse's starting quarterback, Mike Atwood, was eventually benched for freshman Neil Lomax. Lomax would go on to have a prolific college career, breaking all of June's records and becoming the school's all-time leading passer. In fact, by the time he was done at Portland State, Lomax held ninety NCAA records. He later played nine seasons for the St. Louis/Arizona Cardinals.

We held the Vikings' potent offense in check and won the game, 21-12. The 29,949 Hawai'i fans—our largest crowd to date—went home happy.

At this point in the season, our defense was really coming together, especially our secondary. We were developing into the tough, hard-nosed defense that Hawai'i fans had come to expect.

And speaking of hard-nosed:

Pat Schmidt (UH free safety, 1977): *Our team doctor was Herbert Hata. I don't remember what game it was, but our middle linebacker Tom Murphy hit somebody really hard, and Tom's helmet comes off and cuts the bridge of his nose. It was a huge gash.*

So we go in at halftime, and Doctor Hata is trying to stitch up Tom's nose. He grabs a big clump of Tom's skin and inadvertently put a stitch right in there. Tom's shouting, "Doctor! Doctor!" And Doctor Hata, not missing a beat, calmly says, "Don't worry. It's not like you have a future movie career." That was funny! I'm sure to this day, poor Tom still has a big lump on his nose.

On November 5, we played our second and final road game of the season, losing to San Jose State, 24-14. It was a good game, and I thought we competed well. It was a homecoming of sorts for our quarterbacks/receivers coach, Mike Flores. Mike had coached at SJSU before coming over to the Islands prior to the season. Also, Dom Capers, who coached at Hawai'i in 1975 and 1976, was now tutoring the Spartans' secondary. (Dom is currently the defensive coordinator for the Green Bay Packers.)

Our offense struggled in this one, managing only a couple of Curtis Goodman field goals through the first three quarters. The first came in the second quarter. Curtis' 50-yard boot tied our school record for longest field goal. Our only touchdown of the game came in the fourth quarter, when Jeff hit Gerald Green for a 45-yard score.

It was too little, too late.

One Spartan player who really stood out in this contest was linebacker Frank Manumaleuna, whom I recruited when I was at UCLA. At 6-3 and 245 pounds,

Frank was just a monster of a player. When he was a high school senior, all the schools were after him, including USC, Michigan, Nebraska and Oklahoma. His debut at UCLA was one to remember, as he recorded 25 tackles against Tennessee. Unfortunately, he suffered a spine and neck injury during that game, and our Bruins medical staff would not clear him to play again. Frank spent the next two or three years out of football, then got medically cleared at San Jose State. He was an excellent player. His son, Brandon, later played for me at Arizona. Frank's brother, Big John, was recently inducted into the Polynesian Football Hall of Fame.

After the loss to the Spartans, we returned home for a much-appreciated bye week. It came at a great time for us. The bye gave us a chance to get back in the classroom, refresh ourselves and take stock of where we were and how we could get better.

When you have a bye this late in the season, I think it's important to understand that the thing our players need the most is rest. They don't need two-a-day practices or an extra day off. Instead, they need short and quick practices. Just as importantly, they need the coaches to be very specific about what needs to be done to improve as a team.

We were now 3-5 with three games left to play in the season. A winning season, we knew, was within our reach.

The Bowling Green Falcons were our next opponents. They were a solid team that competed in the Mid-American Conference. Their quarterback, Mark Miller, was a talented senior who had started forty-four straight games.

I had a good feeling about this game. The way I look at it, when you have a home game coming off a bye, you should be able to play your best game because you're refreshed and clear about what you need to do. The effort you make in that game should be second to none.

One statistic can summarize how this game went: Miller walked into Aloha Stadium with just six interceptions for the season. We intercepted him six times in this one game.

Scott Voeller, a sophomore linebacker out of Damien High School, picked off Miller twice. Keoni Jardine also had two picks. The first led to a 38-yard touchdown run by George Bell. The second set up an 8-yard Jeff Duva-to-DeWayne Jett hookup for another score. Junior Talaesea and Bryan Hanawahine also came up with big interceptions.

It was just a great night for the team, and for the 28,034 fans in attendance. Keith Hill bulled his way into the end zone for a touchdown. Following a blocked punt by Burton Coloma, tight end Mike Jackson caught a 7-yard touchdown reception from Jeff. And reserve Daryl Edralin, a senior fullback and future UH assistant coach, got into the act with a rushing score of his own.

We won this one going way, 41-21. It was the most points we had scored since the Idaho game.

We were now 4-5 on the year. Up next: South Carolina, one of the preeminent college football programs in the country.

In terms of finances, facilities and other college football benchmarks, the Gamecocks were in a completely different universe than we were. This was a program with all the bells and whistles, and their 1977 squad included a future Heisman Trophy winner in George Rogers.

To make matters worse, South Carolina was coming into this game hungry for redemption because they had just suffered a loss to their bitter state rival, Clemson.

I vividly remember my pre-game conversation with their head coach, Jim Carlen. Carlen had produced the school's first back-to-back winning seasons in nearly a decade, and his 1977 team had fourteen returning starters.

Jim was confident. He had every reason to be.

As I walked around the field during warmups, Jim walked over to me.

"How many players from Hawai'i do you have on your team?" he asked.

"Well, we're going to start nine local players in this game," I responded. "There's a good number of local players here."

"Interesting," he said. "I didn't think there would be that many."

I could not wait to tell our team that the South Carolina head coach thought that we didn't have any players!

Jim started to walk away, and then turned around and said to me, "When this *thang* is over (meaning "slaughter"), give me a call. Our staff will be happy to help you guys. We think you've done a good job, and if we can help you prepare for the next game, we'd love to do that."

It was a nice gesture, but also very condescending. It upset me. I understood that, at the time, people didn't necessarily have a lot of respect for Hawai'i football. Heck, people in the southeast think that they invented football.

Again, I couldn't wait to tell our team what Jim had said.

Final score: Hawai'i 27, South Carolina 7.

It was our biggest and most satisfying win of the season. Dick Fishback of the *Honolulu Advertiser* started his account of the game with, "If Oral Roberts ever wants to look for a miracle worker, he'd better call on a roster-full of University of Hawai'i football players."

The Gamecocks struck first, scoring a touchdown less than four minutes into the game. The Aloha Stadium crowd of 30,146 must have thought, "Uh-oh."

Looking back, however, I think that quick score actually worked to our advantage because it gave South Carolina a false sense of security. They had no idea that it would be their only score of the game.

Again, our defense stepped up in a big way. Linebacker Tom Murphy was spectacular, coming up with 18 tackles. Harris Matsushima had 10 solo tackles from his nose guard position, and 13 in total. Pat Schmidt, who was really blossoming into the leader in the secondary that we needed, contributed 12 stops. Defensive back Burton Coloma had another blocked punt. And Hubbard Martin, a seldom-used defensive lineman, made two huge sacks on Gamecock quarterback Greenham to seal the victory.

Jeff Duva played his best game for us, passing for 123 yards and a 15-yard scoring strike to George Bell. Jeff was really maturing into a great leader for us, using both his passing and running ability to move our offense.

Jack Wright: *I remember that they scored on us in their very first offensive series. They scored a touchdown as if our defense wasn't even there. I thought, "Oh, my God. This is going to be a long night. But we went on to win. Jeff had a hell of a game."*

Jeff Duva: *If we threw the ball twenty-five times a game, that was a lot. We were a smaller, faster team that relied a lot on finesse. I was always more of an option or sprint-out type of quarterback. I liked to run around. At BYU, I kind of felt handcuffed because I always had to stay in the pocket. I loved the offense that we had at Hawai'i because it gave me a lot of flexibility to be creative."*

Greg McElroy (offensive lineman, 1977-78): *The South Carolina game was when we really peaked as a team. We were winning and there were fourteen minutes left. I knew what a win like this would mean for the program. That damn clock wouldn't move fast enough!"*

To this day, I still wonder what kind of help Coach Carlen had in mind for us.

Here's a neat factoid for movie buffs: Ron Bass was the game's starting quarterback for the Gamecocks. This is the same Ron "Sunshine" Bass who inspired the character of the same name in the 2000 film, *Remember the Titans*. The fictional Bass was portrayed by actor Kip Pardue. The real Ron Bass served on the film's creative team.

Our final game of the season was on December 3 against the Arizona Wildcats. It was that school's final game as a member of the Western Athletic Conference. The next year, the Wildcats officially became a member of the expanded Pac-10.

For Hawai'i, it was our chance to have a winning season, a goal that few people—if any—expected us to achieve.

Playing in his final game as a Rainbow Warrior, Curtis Goodman kicked a 42-yard field goal to put us ahead, 3-0, late in the opening quarter. We stopped Arizona cold and got the ball back, but could not move the ball. We were forced to punt, but the snap sailed over the head of our punter, Greg Cummins, and resulted in a safety for the visiting team.

We led 3-2 at the half.

In the second half, Arizona's physicality just took its toll on us. Tony Mason's team was big and strong. They were, by far, the most physical team we had played all year. With our defense worn down, the Wildcats had 325 rushing yards and put the game away, 17-10. Our only touchdown of the game was an 85-yard punt return by Gerald Green early in the fourth quarter.

Our lone bright spot on offense was Jeff Duva. With our ground attack rendered ineffective, Jeff had to throw the ball a lot, and he performed well, completing 13 of 24 passes for 216 yards.

I said it after the game, and I'll say it now: We lost that game in the weight room. We could not match them physically. It all boiled down to Arizona's superior strength. (That would serve as a good lesson for us. We had to find a way to maximize our off-season strength program.)

It was a disappointing end to our season, but I think we came away encouraged by what we had accomplished as a team.

After the game, Ray Nagel invited the coaching staff to his house. Our spirits were down because we wanted to win this game so badly. We were this close to having a winning season.

We were sitting in Ray's Jacuzzi, and Ray said, "You have nothing to feel bad about. You guys did great. Besides, you need to save something for next year!"

A little pragmatism from the boss!

Bob Wagner: *The Arizona game really stands out because we were very competitive against a future Pac-10 team. Afterward, the coaching staff went to Ray Nagel's home in Kāhala. We were in his Jacuzzi, lamenting the fact that we lost the game. Ray said, "That's okay. You guys did a heck of a job this first year. You don't want to have too much success too soon because then the expectations go up that much faster."*

I thought about what Ray said, and I looked around. It was a beautiful setting with palm trees and everything. I thought it was paradise sitting in a Jacuzzi in December, looking at the palm trees. And then to have Ray encourage us like that? I thought, "Wow, Hawai'i really is a special place."

We bid aloha to fourteen seniors in 1977. As expected, Harris Matsushima provided us with leadership on and off the field, finishing the season with 87 tackles. In his only year as a Rainbow Warrior, Pat Schmidt contributed 4 interceptions and 79 total tackles. Tom Murphy, another senior transfer, led our defense with 144 total tackles.

Jeff finished the season with 1,487 passing yards and 10 touchdowns. Wilbert Haslip led our rushing attack, with 698 net yards. Wil was followed closely by Gerald Green (548) and promising freshman George Bell (438). Rick Wagner was our top receiver with 19 receptions. Keoni Jardine led our secondary with 5 interceptions.

Punter Greg Cummins had a fine year for us, with a 41.6-yard average. Curtis Goodman's final season at Hawai'i was solid, with 15 field goals and a perfect 24-for-24 on extra points.

The five months we had just been through were exhilarating and formative for all of us—coaches, players and fans. The people of Hawai'i took to this team in a way that we could never have predicted.

The 1977 season had come to an end. In reality, however, it was just the beginning.

In the next nine years, some of the most epic games, incredible crowds, unforgettable players and coaches, memorable plays and wonderful stories would emanate from Aloha Stadium.

There would be unadulterated joy.

There would be inconsolable heartache.

The people kept coming in greater numbers every year. They kept caring. They kept supporting. They kept living and dying with the Rainbow Warriors.

The fans were connected and wanted to be part of University of Hawai'i football.

This first season was just the preamble of this special generation of Rainbow Warrior football, and that is why it must never be forgotten.

Chapter Four

BUILDING BLOCKS

It was one of those surreal Jack Buck moments. (You know, "I don't believe what I just saw!") And it happened in the home of one of our country's most preeminent heart surgeons.

I don't remember the exact date, but I believe it was a day in January of 1980. Dr. Richard Mamiya, who had played football for the University of Hawai'i in the 1940s, was a tremendous supporter of our program. On occasion, he and his wife, Hazel, would host prospective recruits at their beautiful Hawai'i Kai residence.

On this day, the Mamiyas had invited me and Kaulana Park to their home for breakfast. At the time, Kaulana was one of the premier recruits in the state. The 6-2, 220-pound fullback had led Kamehameha-Kapālama to a pair of Prep Bowl appearances and was part of an outstanding senior class that also included Leroy Lutu (University High), John Kamana (Punahou), Falaniko Noga (Farrington) and Boyd Yap (Kamehameha-Kapālama).

I was locked in on the idea of adding Kaulana to our UH backfield. Stanford was also after him, however, so we were fighting an uphill battle.

Kaulana and I arrived at the Mamiyas' home at our appointed time, and the four of us made some small talk. We made our way to the dining room, where Hazel had already set the table. She went to the kitchen and returned with this enormous tray of breakfast delicacies: bacon, sausage, eggs and so on. I smiled when I saw all that food. A feast was awaiting us!

Hazel put the tray down in front of Kaulana, and we said a blessing for our meal. As soon as we said, "Amen," Kaulana looked straight at Hazel and said, fork in hand, "Wow, this is great. Thank you."

Then he started eating straight off the platter!

The platter of food was meant for the four of us, but Kaulana thought it was all for him. I stared in amazement as he went through the entire platter. Within minutes, he had cleared the entire tray!

Hazel, bless her heart, didn't say a word. She simply returned to the kitchen to prepare more food for the rest of us.

Looking back on our get-together always brings a smile to my face, and I still kid Kaulana about it all the time. Not unexpectedly, he did wind up signing with Stanford and had a productive career there. He later returned to the Islands and has done some great things for our state.

Recruiting. It's been called the lifeblood of any successful college football program. A great recruiting class can lay the foundation for a top-flight program. A poor recruiting class—or too many of them—can send a coach to the unemployment line.

When it comes to recruiting, when a new coach lands at a program, he hits the ground running. That was certainly true when I became the head coach of the Rainbow Warriors. Just days after being hired, I returned to Los Angeles, where Bob Burt called me. I was bringing Bob in to coach our linebackers.

"Coach, I'll pick you up in the morning at four o'clock," he said.

Four o'clock in the morning?

"We have to go recruiting," Bob continued. "Junior Talaesea is getting out of the military today, and he'll be home in Garden Grove. If we can get there early in the morning, we can wake him up and offer him a scholarship."

Junior Talaesea was a 6-1, 250-pound linebacker who had played for Burt at Santiago High School. I had tried to recruit him to UCLA before he joined the Army.

Early-morning wakeup calls aside, recruiting was an undertaking that I relished. I enjoyed recruiting. I know that many other coaches never liked it. They thought that it was an imposition on their time. Many of today's coaches, I'm sure, still regard recruiting as a necessary evil.

I enjoyed recruiting because it was a way to develop great relationships with the players. Even if the player I was recruiting decided to sign with another school (such as Kaulana Park), on many occasions I was able to make a friend for life.

Maybe the best example I can share with you is Gary Carter, the great baseball catcher who starred with the Montreal Expos and New York Mets. When I was at UCLA, I recruited Gary when he was a quarterback at Sunny Hills High School in Fullerton, California. We beat out a hundred other schools to sign Gary, and I was looking forward to see him in Bruin blue and gold. The lure of baseball, however, was too great for him. Gary instead opted to sign a pro contract with the Expos. He would later win a World Series ring with the 1986 Mets, and he was inducted into the Baseball Hall of Fame in 2003. It's safe to say he made a wise choice.

Gary and I remained friends until his passing in 2012. Gary and my son, Rich, were also really good friends.

From the very start of my UH tenure, I emphasized the importance of recruiting local players. Our fans wanted to see the local athletes representing their team. We understood that. We also recognized that Hawai'i was a growing source for Division I football talent. As a result, the number of local players on our UH rosters increased every season during my ten-year stay in the Islands. We had future NFL players like Falaniko Noga, Jesse Sapolu and Rich Miano, but we also brought in guys like Andy Moody, Kesi Afalava, Bryan Almadova, Emlen Kahoano, Amosa Amosa, Michael Beazley, Quentin Flores, Alvis Satele, Doug Nomura, Brian Norwood, Koldene Walsh, Joe Seumalo, Doug Kyle and many other homegrown players.

We also tried to recruit Polynesians or other players who had roots in Hawai'i. These included mainland athletes who had some kind of connection to the Islands. We tried to take advantage of every possible inroad to bringing in players our fans could identify with. If we were going to fail at landing a prospect, we were determined that it wasn't going to be a prospect that lived twenty miles away or even a hundred miles away. That player would live 2,500 miles or even 5,000 miles away. The farther you got away from a recruit, the more difficult it was to make an accurate evaluation of that recruit. After all, you might only get to see them once or twice, maybe three or four times at the most. With a local player, however, you can see him a lot. You can get to know him and his family. So we went after every local hard, even if we didn't have much of a chance to sign him.

I remember recruiting Jesse. He was a player that we thought would be a terrific asset to our program. Standing 6-3 and weighing about 240, Jesse was a tough and agile lineman who starred at Farrington, and it seemed like the whole college football world was trying to get him.

I remember visiting his dad's church. It was a Samoan church on School Street in Honolulu, and I attended one of the services. The sermon was in Samoan, and I didn't understand a word of what was being said. It seemed like the service was going on for a long time, but I just sat there patiently, trying to be respectful. After a time, people began coming and going, and I still sat there waiting for the service to end.

Finally, Jesse's sister walked up to me and said, "Coach, you can leave now. They're going over the financial report."

How embarrassing! There I was, thinking I'm listening to a sermon, when I was actually sitting in on the church's financial report!

Jesse Sapolu (UH offensive lineman, 1979-82): *In those days, you were only allowed to visit five schools. I visited Michigan State, Hawai'i, Oregon, Arizona State and BYU. My decision came down to Arizona State and Hawai'i. After I came back from my Arizona State visit, I pretty much made up my mind that I was going to sign with the Sun Devils. But Coach Tomey paid one more visit to our home. He came and sat on the floor—that was the respectful way in our Samoan culture—and I remember my Dad having him stand up and sit on the couch. Coach's act of respect kind of sold my mother.*

Coach Tomey asked me, "Do you want to go to a program that's already established? Or do you want to stay home and be a part of a group that changes the UH program and brings it to prominence?" At the time, ASU was the No. 2 team in the nation. They had beaten Nebraska the previous season under head coach Frank Kush.

It was a really tough decision and I waited until the very end. Ultimately, Hawai'i was home, and that was important to me.

What makes a good recruiter? This may seem obvious, but a good recruiter is somebody who enjoys people. They like to meet people and get to know them. A good recruiter must be able to be comfortable in all sorts of situations, because every home or school you visit is unique. Sometimes, a recruit may be a tough nut to crack; he may be shy or standoffish or simply hard to get to know. You have to be able to do everything you can to make that young person feel comfortable.

I believed that we needed to teach our coaches how to recruit. It would be wrong to assume that just because someone has been coaching for X number of years that he knows how to recruit the way we want it done. We had people come in and talk to us about how to have conversations with people you aren't familiar with.

George Lumpkin (UH defensive back, 1970-71; UH assistant coach, 1972-95, 1999-2011): *One thing Dick did that was outstanding was to teach us how to recruit. We used to role play. He would bring in people—insurance salesperson, for example—to talk to us about selling and what it means. We'd learn how to talk to people and use key words. Dick also talked to us about learning what other schools were saying about us. What were the negative things that people were saying about our university? By learning those things, we could find ways to combat that. Dick really took our recruiting to a new level.*

I'll never forget this: There was this fellow who was in town for a convention. We got him to talk to us about the art of conversation and how to ask the right questions. He told us, "If you can't think of anything to say, just repeat the last thing the person said, but with a different inflection." In other words, if a recruit tells you, "I don't like math," you could say, "You don't like math?" And that by itself will start a conversation. That simple bit of advice opened a whole new world for us!

As an optimist, I felt that I could get along with anybody. I remember telling our coaches, "You just have to find a way to connect." I believe that the most important attribute that a coach can have is the ability to connect with people—whether it's a recruit, a recruit's parents, his coaches and so on. You have to be able to establish a relationship based on mutual respect.

In those days, every head coach at every high school and junior college in the country had a certain room for recruiters in their office complex. They would tell the recruiter, "Take so-and-so in there." But I instructed my coaches, "Never, ever, ever, ever, ever go in there! If you do, you just become one of the masses." And I firmly believed that. You can sit in that room and talk, and it's uncomfortable. The kid's probably been in there twelve other times with other recruiters. You have to give yourself a chance to stand out from the masses. I encouraged our coaches to take the player for a walk around the school. You could ask, "What's your favorite spot to hang out on campus?" or "Can you introduce me to your favorite teacher?" By doing that, the conversation becomes more relaxed and comfortable. It sure beats sitting in chairs and staring at each other.

We also asked all of our coaches to take recruiting notes. For example, let's say you just made a visit to a recruit's home. You get in your car, drive down to the end of the block, and then you stop to write notes on everything that happened. What were your impressions of the visit? Did the recruit ask a lot of questions? Was his family receptive to the idea of him playing for the University of Hawai'i?

We asked our coaches to keep a file on every recruit. The file had to be so thorough that, if the coach died the next day, someone else could pick up the recruitment without missing a beat. That's how prepared we needed to be.

George Lumpkin: *A lot of times when I went out recruiting, people would say, "Man, I didn't even know the University of Hawai'i had football." Some people think Hawai'i is an easy place to recruit, but it's not. Older people may like the idea of coming here with our beaches and weather, but young guys don't think like that. A lot of recruits thought that Hawai'i was too far away. They thought that NFL teams would never see them play. It was tough.*

With the geographical obstacles that we faced, we weren't going to get many looks from the top-level recruits sought by the likes of USC, Michigan and Notre Dame. For that reason, it was crucial that we identify and target players that were largely overlooked by the big-name schools. We were able to bring in terrific student-athletes because our coaching staff did an outstanding job of talent evaluation.

Walter Murray is an excellent example of an under-the-radar player who came to Hawai'i and did great things for us. Walter, a 6-4, 190-pound wide receiver out of Berkeley, California, was primarily known as a track star. In fact, he had set the national high school record in the 300-meter hurdle.

Walter Murray (UH wide receiver, 1982-85): *From the hills in Berkeley, you can see the whole Bay Area, and the marina side looks just like a Hawai'i volcano. I was sitting there with my girlfriend, and we were listening to the radio. They were promoting some kind of contest where the winner would go to Hawai'i.*

I said, "I'm going to Hawai'i one day." Later on, when the UH coaches contacted me, I thought, "Wow. I really am going to Hawai'i!"

I remember the first time I got into a UH game. Bernard Quarles was the quarterback. Coach Tomey told me the play, and I ran from the sideline to the huddle. About halfway, though, I looked up and saw 50,000 people looking at me. I just stopped and did a complete circle. Everybody was yelling and screaming at me. I finally got to the huddle, and Bernard said, "What's the play?" I had completely forgotten the play! I just said, "I don't know." That was my first play ever at UH!

Our coaching staff had one standing rule: If you visit our campus and our players don't like you, then we're done. I don't care if you're the best player we've ever seen. If you don't get along with our players, we're done recruiting you. We did that several times at UH. One of our players would come to us and report, "Coach, wow, is he selfish!" or "Wow, this guy's a jerk." We don't want our players to have to put up with that.

Bringing in the right kind of person is maybe even more important than bringing in the right kind of athlete. My old coach Bo Schembechler used to say, "If you recruit a guy hard and you get him, then you have him every day for four or five years. If it's the wrong guy, he can kill your program." And Bo was right. If you turn away a recruit who's a good athlete but has poor character, conceivably he might hurt you once a year for four years. But if you sign that same recruit, he will hurt you every day for those four years. You want to avoid bad fits.

We also didn't make promises to our recruits. I just don't think that's the right way to do it. You have to present an honest approach. If you start giving away starting positions in the living room, you're not going to be successful in the long run. Some coaches do that, and it just doesn't work. People have long memories. They are going to remember you if you try to pull the wool over their eyes.

When I re-recruited Blane Gaison before my first season at UH, he wanted to play quarterback. The easy thing would've been for me to tell him, "Okay, you're going to be our quarterback." But I had no idea if he could be our quarterback. I had never seen Blane play. What I saw in Blane was a young man who was a good person, a realistic person and a winner.

I told him, "I don't know if you're a quarterback. I don't know what your best position is. The only thing I know is that we're going to put together a really terrific program, and we're going to have a great chance to win.

"If you're the best quarterback, you'll play. If not, you'll play another position. I cannot make any promises to you. We're going to give everybody an opportunity."

I'd say Blane worked out pretty well for us. After graduating from UH, he played four seasons with the NFL's Atlanta Falcons—as a safety—and went on to become one of Hawai'i's most respected high school coaches and administrators.

A lot of times, recruits were more interested in getting a free trip to Hawai'i than in actually playing for us. The coaches developed a sixth sense in terms of recruits who intended to "trip" us, but it helped to have other tools at our disposal.

We occasionally used third-party calls to talk to recruits on the mainland. We would ask a friend to give a player a call, or sometimes we'd even masquerade as another recruiter. (In those days, remember, phones didn't have caller ID.) We'd pretend to be a coach at Texas Tech or some other school that was far away. We'd ask the player what schools he was planning to visit, and sometimes he would respond with, "Well, I'm visiting Hawai'i next weekend, but I'm not actually interested in them." Then we'd cancel the trip. Other times, we used these third-party calls to get feedback on how we were doing with certain recruits. As I like to say, "Feedback is the breakfast of champions!"

Technically, my first recruiting class at the University of Hawai'i was the 1977 group. We brought in some talented players that year, including George Bell, Burton Coloma, Keoni Jardine, Nelson Maeda, Walt Little, Semeri Ulufale and Junior Talaesea. But remember, I was hired just weeks before the start of the season, and we didn't have the benefit of a comprehensive recruiting effort. That is why I consider 1978 to be my first full recruiting class.

And, oh my goodness, what a class it was.

Gary Allen (UH running back, 1978-81): *I had a couple of other opportunities with other schools, but once I visited Hawai'i, that was it. I fell in love with the sheer beauty of Hawai'i.*

I was recruited as a wide receiver, but I played both receiver and running back in high school. I remember my first year at UH. The running backs and receivers had separate meeting rooms, and I remember walking by the running backs room and telling the coaches that I wanted to be a running back. I said that I could do all the things that they wanted their backs to do. But they didn't believe me because I was so light at the time. Besides, they already had a bunch of good running backs, guys like Wilbert Haslip, George Bell and David Toloumu.

Gary Allen was from Baldwin Park High School in California. He was small—5-9 and 165 pounds—but tremendously quick and strong. We recruited him as a wide receiver, but we knew that it was very likely that he could eventually be a running back. We just thought it was going to take time for him to develop the strength he needed.

One day in practice midway through the 1978 season, all of our running backs went down. I said, "Gary, get in there. Play tailback for a couple of plays and let's see what you can do."

Gary Allen: *There were maybe twenty minutes left in practice. The coaches were going to put in Nathan Fletcher, who was one of our linebackers. They said, "Let's finish up with Nathan." But Coach Tomey said, "No. Gary says he can do it. Let's give him a try."*

On my first attempt, Nathan sacked me. On my second attempt, I got the ball and went from the 50 to the 2-yard line. And the coaches said, "Okay, Gary's going to be a running back." (Laughs)

I mean, wow. Nobody could tackle him. He ran for a touchdown. I said, "Let's do it again the other way," and he ran for another touchdown. It was crazy. Gary made everybody look like that were running in slow motion. He had such great feet, quickness and an instinct with the ball. We were all standing there dumbfounded because we had a great tailback on our team and didn't know it.

Gary made his official debut as our running back against Pacific. It was our homecoming game, and he ran for 92 yards on 20 carries. We lost the game, but Gary was well on his way to becoming Hawaiʻi's all-time leading rusher, with 3,451 yards. (That record might never be broken. Quarterback Michael Carter is second on the all-time list, more than 900 yards behind Gary.)

Another freshman from our 1978 class who made a big impact for us was David Toloumu, a running back from Oceanside, California. David was a tough, physical guy who could just make plays for us. He was very versatile and talented, and bigger than Gary. He started out as a tailback but, as Gary ascended to claim that position, David eventually settled in as our starting fullback.

David Toloumu (UH running back, 1978-81): *I took visits to Oregon, Washington, Colorado, Hawaiʻi, USC and San Jose State. I chose Hawaiʻi because of Mosi Tatupu, the great USC fullback who was on his way to the NFL. He was my host, and he advised me to go where I could play right away as a freshman. Coach Tomey told me that they weren't afraid to play freshmen. He said that he believed that I could play as a freshman because of my speed.*

Man, living in Hawaiʻi was a big adjustment for me. Coming from California, where everything is go, go, go, it seemed everything stayed in first gear in Hawaiʻi. The lifestyle in Hawaiʻi was so slow, like walking in mud. I got homesick that first year. Our first game was against New Mexico, and I didn't play a single down. It was the first time since my Pop Warner days that I sat out an entire game. I started out as the sixth-string tailback. But little by little, I started moving up the depth chart. By the third game I was playing regularly.

Then there's Dana McLemore, who had four outstanding seasons for us as both a cornerback and punt returner. How we signed Dana is a pretty good story—a story that, until I started writing this book, I was completely in the dark about.

George Lumpkin: *Yeah, Dick didn't know this story. Nobody was really recruiting Dana at the time. I found out later that other schools visited him, but he just wasn't interested. I remember talking to his high school coach, and he said, "This guy can do it all. He's not real big, but he can run and he can defend."*

When I looked at Dana's film, it was unbelievable. He could run, catch and change direction with ease. I returned to Hawai'i and told our coaches about Dana. I told them how good this guy is, and that we really needed to sign him.

The thing was, Bob Burt was going after this other defensive back, a guy named Tim Coleman. San Diego State was also trying to get Tim. So one day, me, Dick and Ed Kezirian were driving in Los Angeles. Now, Dick loved Ed because Ed had played for him at UCLA. Ed was an outstanding person and a very good coach, and I see why Dick really liked him. But Ed and I were close, too. We knew each other well because we had recruited the same areas.

So we're driving, and Dick says, "George, I'm not sure we're going to be able to sign Dana."

What? I was flabbergasted. How could we possibly pass on a guy like Dana?

"Bob's got this other DB out in Orange County, Tim Coleman," Dick said. San Diego State is after him, too. We can't sign both of them. If we get Tim, we're not going to be able to sign Dana."

So we're driving along, and Dick spots a phone booth. He says, "Ed, pull over here so I can talk to Bob. I want to see how he's doing with Tim." As Dick jumps out of the car to use the phone, I lean over to Ed and say, "If Dick comes back and tells us that things aren't going too well with Tim Coleman, you need to tell him that we should go ahead and sign Dana. We can't pass up a guy like Dana."

Dick gets back in the car, and he's frowning. "I don't know, guys. Bob says it might be tough signing Tim."

So Ed says, "You know what, Dick? I think we ought to go ahead and sign Dana McLemore. We need a DB, and if it looks like Tim is leaning toward San Diego State, then we need to get Dana."

Dick paused for a moment. And then he said, "That's right. That's right. George, go ahead and tell Dana that he has a scholarship."

I said, "Ed, take me to my car right now!" I knew I had to find Dana right away. One thing about Dick: He is a man of his word. So I wanted to make sure that I got to Dana before Dick changed his mind or found out that Tim was coming. I went right over to Venice High School, found Dana and gave him the news.

"Dana, you've got a scholarship to the University of Hawai'i!"

The funny thing is that Tim also ended up coming to Hawai'i. But he wasn't close to being of Dana's caliber. So that's the Dana McLemore story.

Dana, David and Gary were three pillars of our 1978 class, and all three would go on to play in the NFL: Dana earned a Super Bowl ring with the San Francisco 49ers, Gary played for the Houston Oilers and Dallas Cowboys, and David had a stint with the Atlanta Falcons (reuniting with Blane Gaison).

Of course, they weren't the only contributors in that class. Our 1978 recruiting efforts also brought in talented young men like Keith Ah Yuen out of Kamehameha-Kapālama, Nathan Fletcher from Waianae, Andrew Moody from Waipahu and Peter Kim from Kaiser. Mainland imports included the likes of Itai Sataua, Marcus Tarver, Steve Lehor, Verlon Redd and Tony Holyfield.

When it comes to recruiting, you usually lose more than you win. I've always said that, over my entire coaching career, if the guys we signed played the guys who got away, the guys who got away would win by a lopsided score. That's just the reality of the coaching profession.

I didn't mind missing out on a guy as long as we worked hard in competing for him. There was always a chance that he might join our program later. (Mark Tuinei and Kani Kauahi are two examples of big-time local players who joined us after starting their college careers on the mainland.) At the very worst, I'd know that I made a friend for life.

Leroy Lutu is a good example. We worked so hard to recruit Leroy, who was a standout receiver at Pac-Five. When he signed with the University of Washington, I needed about a month to get over it. I think that's understandable. You spend two years recruiting a guy, only to lose him in the end. When you lose a game, you have another game the following week, so you're forced to put the loss behind you quickly. With recruiting, the sting lingers for a while.

In the case of Kurt Gouveia, I don't think I'll ever get over it.

One of the biggest mistakes of my football life was how I bungled my evaluation of Kurt. I did the worst job imaginable. I didn't think he could contribute to our team. I didn't view him as linebacker material.

Was I ever wrong. Kurt, who played for the great Larry Ginoza at Waianae High School, was interested in coming to UH. But because we didn't return the interest, he went to Brigham Young, where he became a star linebacker for the Cougars' 1984 championship team. He would later win two Super Bowl championships with the Washington Redskins.

Kurt and I are both at peace with the situation now, but it took us a couple of decades for the wounds to heal. Kurt was really hard on us. He wanted to beat us badly, and he did. He recruited against us. And I don't blame him one bit.

One player that I did make a hard push for was Louis Santiago out of Kahuku. It was 1981 and Louis was considered the top back in the state. A lot of the guys from the North Shore ended up going to BYU because of the Mormon church, and our coaching staff agonized over whether we could get Louis or not.

Louis spent a lot of time with us the summer before his senior year, so we felt we were in good shape with him. We heard that he really liked UH but was not ready to make a commitment. We wanted him in our program so much, and waiting for his decision was pure torture.

So one day in early December, Louis comes to our campus to see us, and he and I start talking. During the course of our conversation, he lets me know that he's decided to be a Rainbow Warrior. I was so excited, I wanted to bounce off the walls of our office and call our coaches! Then I asked him, "Louis, when did you decide that you wanted to come to UH?"

Louis gave me this quizzical look, closed one eye and looked up in the air.

"Oh, I think it was September," he said nonchalantly.

I could have killed him!

Louis (who now goes by Keala) ended up being a really good player for us.

Over time, we began to identify certain recruiting areas that brought us a lot of success. Washington state, for instance, brought us the Kafentzis brothers, Lyndell Jones, John Taylor and M.L. Johnson, all of whom made great contributions to our program. We also expanded our recruiting reach outside of the U.S., procuring players from Samoa, Australia, New Zealand and Canada.

In 1983, we signed Colin Scotts, a 6-5, 265-pound defensive lineman from Sydney, Australia. Rich Ellerson did a great job of recruiting him. Football was a completely new experience for Colin, who was a terrific rugby player. He didn't understand why football players needed to wear all the pads. And he didn't understand why football teams didn't follow rugby tradition by meeting in the middle of the field after the game to enjoy some adult beverages. (A little trivia for you: Colin was the first player from Australia to receive a football scholarship in the U.S. He was also the first Australian to be drafted in the NFL.)

Colin was able to learn the game of football fairly quickly. He had great pride, loved to compete and had a motor that wouldn't quit. Even better, because he had no experience playing football, Colin had no bad habits. He was also a delight to be around, always greeting teammates and coaches with, "G'day, mate!"

Colin later had a brief stint with the NFL's St. Louis Cardinals. He could have had a much longer professional career, but the lure of home was too great.

This chapter wouldn't be complete without mentioning three of the great families that represented our program with such distinction.

The contributions of the Goeas brothers, for example, spanned almost my entire coaching tenure at Hawai'i. Larry was the first, joining us as a walk-on in 1978.

John came on board in 1981 as a wide receiver, although he later transitioned to linebacker. And the youngest brother, Leo, joined our program in 1985.

Larry Goeas (UH defensive lineman/linebacker, 1979-82): *From 1978 to 1989, there was a Goeas on the team. It was a good time, and our Dad just loved it. He was so proud of us. Of course, Leo was the highly recruited brother. He and Bern Brostek were the two recruits that everybody wanted.*

When Leo signed with us, he wanted to be a tight end. When fall camp started, I was watching him practice. He was a terrific athlete. But later on, at mealtime, I noticed he wasn't eating very much. It turned out that Leo was afraid of putting on weight. He was *this close* to being an offensive tackle. As the days went on, we finally made the decision as a coaching staff that we needed Leo to switch to tackle. Instead of taking the news hard, he got very excited. He could eat again!

The move paid off for him. Leo went on to play eight seasons in the NFL.

From 1980 through 1987, the name "Noga" struck fear into the hearts of opposing offenses. Niko, Pete and Al all made significant contributions to our program. All three would later play in the NFL.

Niko was the first. Although he wasn't very tall, he had scary ability. Playing both nose guard and linebacker, Niko was selected All-WAC in all four seasons he competed for us. Pete, the middle brother, was a hard-hitting linebacker who was tough as nails. And until Colt Brennan became a Heisman Trophy candidate in 2007, Al was the most decorated Rainbow Warrior in school history. The "Samoan Sack Man" earned All-American honors from the Associated Press in 1986.

Falaniko Noga (UH defensive lineman/linebacker, 1980-83): *I chose Hawai'i because I wanted to play in front of my family. That was important to me. Coach Tomey told me, "If you want to be the best, you have to work hard and do your job right." And I thought, "I can do that." I never tried to be a superstar, but I did everything I could to prove myself on the football field. I never took anything for granted, and I was willing to take on any challenge.*

I didn't know if my younger brothers would follow me [to Hawai'i], although we used to talk about it when we were growing up. I used to tell them, "If anyone is going to push us to do better, it has to be us." Together, we made a name for ourselves. When Al became an All-American, the first thing that came to my mind was, "Thank God." It was God that gave him that talent.

Finally, no family has contributed more players to UH football than the Kafentzis 'ohana. Eight Kafentzis boys wore the green and white: Mark, Kent, Kurt, Kyle, Sean, Landon, Mikhail and Tyson. Their entire family was just tremendous.

Mark Kafentzis (UH defensive back, 1980-81): *During my recruitment, Coach Tomey never came to visit my house, so I never knew what he looked like. On my recruiting visit, Coach Wagner was showing me around. He introduced me to Coach Tomey, and I said, "What position do you coach?" That was funny!*

I did have somewhat of a UH connection: My junior college coach, Dick Zornes, had coached at UH under Dave Holmes. I also had a cousin in Hawai'i who was in the Marines.

When I went to UH, that basically opened the gates for the rest of the family. I remember when the twins, Kent and Kurt, came over. Kurt got really homesick. He kept calling our mom every day. Finally, she told him, "Hey, if you want to come home, then join the Army and get transferred over here. Otherwise, you're sticking it out in Hawai'i!"

As the seasons passed, not only were we able to bring in a lot of great players to our program, but we also added some top-level coaches as well. Doug Kay, for example, was our defensive coordinator for three seasons (1981 to 1983). Doug was one of the best coaches that we ever had here, and we all learned a lot from him. He later became a head coach in the Arena Football League; in fact, he's now with the Tampa Bay Storm as their defensive coordinator.

Dave Fagg was our associate head coach and offensive coordinator from 1979 to 1981 and 1983 to 1986. He was an invaluable help to us because of his maturity and previous head coaching experience at Davidson College. Dave and I coached at Davidson together, and he remains my closest friend in the coaching profession. He used to introduce himself to the players by saying, "I'm Dave Fagg. That's F-A-G-G!" The players loved that!

In 2015, Dave, who was once named Davidson's top athlete, was inducted into his alma mater's Athletics Hall of Fame.

Adam Rita spent three seasons with us as our wide receivers coach (1979 to 1981) and then another year as our offensive coordinator. Adam was a local boy from Kaua'i (as a boy, he appeared in the Elvis Presley film, *Blue Hawaii*), and he was thrilled to be back home after coaching stints at Boise State and UNLV. Following our 1982 season, Adam joined the B.C. Lions of the Canadian Football League as the team's offensive coordinator. In 1991, as the head coach of the Toronto Argonauts, Adam led his team to the Grey Cup title.

Next to Bob Wagner and George Lumpkin, the coach with the longest tenure on my Hawai'i staff was Daryl Edralin (1979 to 1986). Daryl was a running back on our 1977 team, and served as a G.A. for us the following year. He was a great running backs coach at UH and helped develop the talents of guys like Gary Allen, David Toloumu, Anthony Edgar, Nu'u Fa'aola and Heikoti Fakava.

In 1984, we were fortunate enough to bring in Larry MacDuff as our linebackers and special teams coach. He was a tremendous coach who later served as my defensive coordinator at Arizona. Larry also enjoyed a lengthy coaching stint in the NFL.

And then there's Duane Akina, who joined our staff in 1981 as a volunteer assistant and went on to coach linebackers and defensive backs for us through the 1985 season. Duane, who played quarterback at Punahou School and the University of Washington, ended up being an exceptional defensive coach. He was also part of my staff at Arizona and is now the defensive backs coach at Stanford. He's the only coach that I know of who was both an offensive coordinator and defensive coordinator in the Pac-12.

I also got to work with Duane in 2004 when I was part of Mack Brown's staff at Texas. Duane was on the Longhorns' staff for fourteen seasons. In my mind, it's really unfortunate that Duane never got the opportunity to be a head coach somewhere. He's as fine a head coaching prospect as I've ever seen.

UH football also has a proud history of players who joined the program as walk-ons, and I'll address that subject in a later chapter. But from Blane Gaison and Gary Allen to Niko Noga and Jesse Sapolu, there is no question that we were blessed to have so many great student-athletes donning Rainbow Warrior uniforms.

And with powerhouse schools like USC, Michigan, Nebraska and Wisconsin on our schedules, we would need every single one of them.

Chapter Five

SLAYING THE GIANTS

"When Goliath came against the Israelites, the soldiers all thought, 'He is so big. We can never kill him.' David looked at the same giant and thought, 'He is so big. I can't miss.'"

– Russell Johnston, Scottish legislator

"We didn't care if it was Oklahoma or Iowa or Nebraska. Our thing was, 'When you guys come here to play us, we're going to kick your ass.'"

– Brian Derby, Hawai'i Rainbow Warrior

Ask any knowledgeable sports fan to list college football's perennial powers, and the response will generally include these names: USC, Michigan, Nebraska, Oklahoma, Wisconsin, Arizona State, Iowa, West Virginia and South Carolina. These programs were led by some of the game's coaching giants, such as Bo Schembechler, Barry Switzer, Tom Osborne, Hayden Fry and John Robinson. These schools also featured Heisman Trophy winners Marcus Allen, Charles White and Mike Rozier, as well as future NFL All-Pros like Ronnie Lott, Roger Craig, Irving Fryar and Nate Odomes.

What do these schools, coaches and players have in common? They all competed against the University of Hawai'i during my ten-year stay in Manoa.

While we didn't slay every one of these traditional gridiron giants, we beat enough of them to gain the respect of the college football world. Just as importantly, we were able to capture the imagination of the tens of thousands of Hawai'i fans who came to Aloha Stadium to see their team take on the true Goliaths of college football. The fans seemed to buy into the mantra we had established for ourselves as a team: "BELIEVE, BELIEVE, BELIEVE!"

I loved playing these big games. Most of these contests took place at home at the end of the season, so they gave our fans something special to look forward to. These games also gave us a chance to test ourselves against the nation's most successful football programs.

We could—and did—beat some of these schools. I told our players over and over again: The best team doesn't always win. It's the team that plays best that wins. There's a hell of a difference between the two. Football games aren't beauty contests. They're not about who's bigger or faster or stronger. The games are decided on who plays best, who doesn't turn the ball over and who makes the right plays in the fourth quarter. All of those things are magnified in the biggest games you play.

Jesse Sapolu: *Everyone in Hawai'i kept hearing about how great Nebraska or Oklahoma was, or how great South Carolina or West Virginia was. We wanted to show our fans that, hey, we can beat these guys. So playing in these games was exciting for me.*

Nu'u Fa'aola (UH running back, 1982-85): *They're human beings like we are. The only difference between the two teams was the uniforms. That's it. I know people see these schools play on TV all the time, so they become a bigger thing. For me, when I played, the only things that were important to me were my teammates and the uniform on my back. Am I doing my part? Am I blocking the right guy? Am I making the right play? I never worried about who we played. I was too busy trying to win the game.*

Brian Derby (UH offensive lineman, 1982-85): *We looked forward to those games. The bigger, the better.*

I recounted our 1977 games against South Carolina and Arizona in an earlier chapter. The Gamecocks and Wildcats were early tests for our growing program, but the challenges only got more imposing as the years went on.

In the second game of the 1978 season, for example, we traveled to Lincoln, Nebraska to take on coaching legend Tom Osborne and his No. 10-ranked Nebraska Cornhuskers.

We were coming off a season-opening victory over New Mexico, and were eager to test our mettle against one of college football's traditional powers. We were big underdogs heading into the game, and rightly so. The Cornhuskers had just rebounded from a stinging loss at Alabama with a decisive win over Cal.

Jack Wright: *We were so jet lagged. The night before the game, we went to bed at midnight, which was still seven o'clock in Hawai'i. We couldn't sleep. Basically, it was like playing a football game at eight in the morning in Hawai'i. It was a tough way to play a game.*

I remember going out to the stadium for practice on Friday. Nebraska was coming off the field, and they were in full pads. These guys were huge. I said, "What are these guys doing, practicing in full pads the day before the game?" And some guy standing next to me goes, "Oh, that's the jayvee team." Oh, my gosh!

At this stage of our program, we were not ready to play the likes of Nebraska. And the results proved that. The Cornhuskers handed it to us, 56-10.

We kept it close for a while. We trailed just 7-0 at the end of the first quarter, and we were moving the ball to open the second stanza. We committed a couple of mistakes on special teams, however, and after that it was like fighting a snowball rolling down a hill. The deficit kept growing and growing.

Senior fullback Wilbert Haslip led our running attack with 66 yards on 12 carries. Jeff Duva struggled a bit at quarterback, passing for only 92 yards, but in his defense he was running for his life for almost the entire game. Our lone touchdown was an 11-yard strike from Jeff to receiver Wayne Black.

The Cornhuskers were led by the ingeniously named Isaiah Moses Hipp—"I.M. Hipp"—who rushed for 70 yards and a touchdown.

"We have to look at the positive aspects of all this," I said after the game. "For one thing, a lot of players got into this game. We found some guys that will make us better." (I wasn't kidding. All but two players on our sixty-man travel roster participated in the contest.)

David Toloumu: *I was stunned seeing 75,000 people screaming at us. It was a sea of red. They booed us as we ran onto the field, and [the booing] felt like it vibrated to my very soul. That was pretty intimidating for us. We got crushed."*

In our 1978 season finale, we hosted the USC Trojans. John Robinson was their coach at the time, and the Trojans were coming off a big 27-25 win over Joe Montana and the Notre Dame Fighting Irish. The Men of Troy came to Honolulu ranked No. 3 in the country and were very much in contention for the national championship.

Quite simply, USC was loaded. Their star tailback was Charles White, who, still in his junior season, had already passed Mike Garrett, O.J. Simpson, Ricky Bell and Anthony Davis as his school's career rushing leader. White's backup was a hungry young freshman named Marcus Allen. The Trojans' offensive line was led by future NFL players Keith Van Horne and Brad Budde. (Their best lineman, future Hall of Fame player Anthony Munoz, was out of action with an arm injury.)

The USC defense was bolstered by defensive backs Ronnie Lott and Dennis Smith, along with linebacker Riki Gray (later known as Riki Ellison).

But the Rainbow Warriors were up for the challenge. With a 6-4 record, we had already clinched a winning season. It would be the final game for seniors Jeff Duva, Chris Johnston, Jack Wright, Kevin Scullion, Greg McElroy, Tom Clark, Mike Jackson, Walt Little, Gary Spotts, Mike Arvanetis, Hubbard Martin, Joe Panora, Arthur Smith, Scott Voeller, Greg Cummins and Bryan Hanawahine. Another senior, Wilbert Haslip, was lost for the year after injuring his knee in our fifth game of the season, a somber 25-11 win over San Jose State. (Despite missing our final six games, Wil was named our team's MVP at the end of the season.)

Saturday, December 2. For UH fans, it would be a night to remember.

The first score of the game was a 37-yard field goal by Peter Kim, our freshman placekicker out of Kaiser High School, midway through the first quarter. Bryan Hanawahine recovered a USC fumble just five plays into the game to set up Peter's kick. USC responded with Charles White running off tackle for an 18-yard score.

Bryan Hanawahine: *You know, most coaches, when you play a big game, they try to get you all fired up. But with Coach Tomey, we did everything the same that week. Nothing changed. All he said was, "We have to believe we can beat them. Nobody else thinks we have a chance." A bunch of us local players looked at each other and said, "Eh, does he know who we playing, or what? They're the No. 1 team in the freakin' country!"*

But Coach taught us to believe in ourselves, and he got us to buy in. I will never forget this game.

Neither team scored in the second quarter, and the Trojans led at halftime, 7 to 3. The 48,767 fans (a new Aloha Stadium attendance record) were going crazy. The home fans were smelling an upset!

Our defense was incredible. Linebacker Scott Voeller had the game of his life, coming up with 20 tackles. He was all over the field. Cornerback Burton Coloma and linebacker Junior Talaesea each contributed 12 tackles.

The third quarter was more of the same. Our defense would not budge. We even used an eight-man front at times to stop White from running wild on us. Still, White rushed for 152 yards in the game on 31 carries. (After the game was over, White admitted that he hadn't expected to play that much against Hawai'i. "I never thought I'd wind up carrying the ball 31 times," he told reporters afterward. "I didn't think I'd even play in the second half.")

At the start of the final quarter, the game remained USC 7, Hawai'i 3. Right away, we caught a break when the Trojans snapped the ball out of their end zone. The resulting safety inched us even closer, 7-5.

A play that many UH fans still talk about was David Toloumu's halfback pass to Jeff Duva. We were moving the ball down the field, and we had some momentum on our side. The time was right for a trick play.

Jeff Duva: *We had worked on that play all week. We were saving it for a big moment during the game. Everything came down to the fourth quarter, and we* *were driving on USC. We called the play. I pitched the ball to our tailback, David Toloumu, and I snuck out to the left side of the field, near the sideline. I was wide open. David threw this high, floating rainbow pass—no pun intended—and I had to get on my horse to get to it. All I was saying to myself when I saw the ball in the air was, "I got to get to it! I got to get to it! We're going to win if I catch this!" I got to the ball, and I think I shocked myself. The ball hit my hands and bounced right off.*

I remember going back to the huddle after that play. Jack Wright looked at me and said, "Nice hands."

Jack Wright: *Jeff and I still joke about it all the time. I always remind him about it. I tell him, "Is there any way we can go back in time, and you catch that pass this time?" I mean, it was crazy. We had a sold-out crowd, and the place was so loud. But after Jeff dropped the ball, there was just dead silence. It was the first time I could hear everything in the huddle. Jeff had this blank look on his face. I just said, "Nice hands, Jeff." I wanted to break the ice and get everyone to laugh.*

David Toloumu: *Yeah, we still talk about it. When Jeff sees me, he starts nodding his head. I just open my arms wide, like, "I can't believe you still even think about that!" Hey, we almost upset USC. We gave them a good game. Watching Gary Allen run past those USC guys, I began to think, "We can play with these guys. We can do this!"*

Jeff Duva: *What everybody forgets is that after that play we ran a trap option, where I faked the pitch and ran for a first down. We had first and ten at about the 20-yard line. Then I completed a pass over the middle to the 5-yard line. Our receiver got sandwiched between Ronnie Lott and Dennis Smith and coughed up the ball. Nobody remembers that. They all remember the dropped pass.*

It's true. Jeff still gets teased about dropping the pass. Looking at the film, there was no one on that side of the field except for Jeff. But nobody was upset at him. Nobody wanted to win that game more than Jeff did. In the end, it was just one play, and it didn't cost us the game.

USC scored two touchdowns near the end of the game to win, 21-5.

After the game, Coach Robinson knew his team had barely escaped what would have been a monumental upset. I know he wasn't happy with the officiating—the Trojans had 157 yards in penalties—but he was quick to give our team credit.

"The story of this game was Hawaiʻi," he told *Honolulu Advertiser* writer Ferd Lewis. "They played hard. Give them credit. They blitzed us. They played just a great game."

USC went on to defeat Michigan in the Rose Bowl, earning a share of college football's national championship (sharing the mythical title with Alabama, which they had beaten at Legion Field in Birmingham earlier in the season).

Jeff Duva: *USC came to Honolulu thinking they were on vacation. But Coach Tomey got us ready, and we went out there and played our hearts out. It probably would have been the biggest upset in college football history had we pulled it off. That USC team was probably one of the greatest college football teams of all time, and we took them right down to the wire.*

Greg Cummins (UH P, 1977-78): *In 1975, when I was at Cal, we beat USC when they were national champions. When Hawaiʻi played the Trojans in 1978, we didn't have anywhere near the team that Cal had. But we played with emotion. We were playing like brothers. It was an exciting game, and we almost pulled it out. Looking back, even though we lost, it was probably the highlight of my college football career. That game stands above [Cal's victory] because of what we did as a team and the unity that we had. I never felt anything like it.*

We hosted another Pac-10 power in the final game of our 1979 campaign: The Arizona State Sun Devils.

ASU was coached by the legendary Frank Kush. The former Army lieutenant was a fixture in Tempe, having served as their head coach since 1958. Kush was renowned as a stern disciplinarian who got the most out of his players. "Mount Kush," a steep, sun-scorched hill located near the Sun Devils' practice facility, served as a foreboding presence for his players. Any player that required discipline would have to run up and down that hill numerous times.

At the start of the 1979 season, however, a former Sun Devil player sued the school, accusing Kush and his staff of mental and physical harassment. On October 13, three hours before ASU's game against No. 6-ranked Washington, Kush was fired for allegedly interfering with the school's internal investigation into the allegations. The veteran coach was allowed to coach that game, and the Sun Devils pulled off an emotional upset over the Huskies.

ASU boasted a strong football tradition. Former Sun Devils include gridiron greats such as Charley Taylor, Curley Culp, Danny White, Mike Haynes and John Jefferson. Before switching to baseball, Reggie Jackson played a season of football at ASU.

By this time, however, we were more physically and mentally prepared to take on college football's big boys. We were 5-5, and our senior class, led by Tom Tuinei, Jerry Scanlan, Jeff Cabral, Nicky Clark, Burton Coloma, Beldon Kealoha and Wayne Black, wanted to go out with a second consecutive winning season.

The game didn't start out very well. On just the second play from scrimmage, ASU halfback Robert Weathers sprinted 77 yards for a touchdown. He ran right past our bench. In the second quarter, the Sun Devils added a field goal to make the score 10-0.

Then our offense, led by our quarterback, Blane Gaison, went to work.

That's right. *Quarterback* Blane Gaison.

Since being injured in the first game of our 1977 season, Blane had found success as our starting free safety. But the week before our ASU game, we were in a real struggle against Colorado State. We were down, 10-3, at halftime. Our starting quarterback, Mike Stennis, was out with an injury, and his backup, Steve Rakhshani, wasn't able to get our offense going. A change had to be made.

> **Blane Gaison:** *As we were running into the locker room at halftime, Coach Tomey grabbed me by the arm, pulled me aside and said, "I need you to play quarterback." I looked at him and said, "Are you serious?"*
>
> *"Yes," he said. So I said, "Okay." And that was it. You just did what Coach wanted you to do, no questions asked. We drew up about three or four plays in the locker room, and we ran those plays in the second half and wound up winning the game. It was a surprise for the Rams, I'm sure. Even my parents came up to me after the game and asked me, "What happened?"*

Blane did a great job for us against Colorado State, and we won the game, 24-10. Blane didn't throw the ball very much—he was 2 for 4 for 31 passing yards—but he had 8 carries for 78 rushing yards. More than anything, he gave us great leadership.

We stuck with Blane as our quarterback for the ASU game, and he again came through for us, scampering for 3 touchdowns and directing our explosive rushing attack. Gary Allen, now established as an All-WAC performer, was nearly unstoppable against the Sun Devils. He ran for 155 yards and became just the third UH player to amass more than 1,000 yards in a season.

> **Gary Allen:** *The Arizona State game was one of my favorites. I had a buddy who played at ASU, Ron Brown. He was an Olympic 4 x 100 sprinter, and he and I went to high school together. He called me before the game and talked some trash, saying, "We're going to stop you and shut you down." That really motivated me.*

Fellow super-soph David Toloumu added 58 yards on the ground, and senior fullback Keith Hill chipped in with 62 yards. Even our punter, Jim Asmus, got into the act, running a third-quarter fake punt for 21 yards and a big first down. All told, our offense generated a whopping 353 rushing yards!

After ASU's early lead, our defense pretty much shut down their offense. In the third quarter, we forced a fumble by future NFL running back Gerald Riggs, and freshman defensive tackle Kesi Afalava recovered the ball, setting up a Jim Asmus field goal. Later, another future NFL player, quarterback Mark Malone, coughed up the pigskin during a pass attempt, and sophomore defensive lineman Itai Sataua plucked the ball out of mid-air for another costly ASU turnover.

One of the biggest plays of the game was a "reverse muddle huddle." Earlier in the contest, we ran a muddle huddle play, where quarterback Mike Stennis crouched next to the ball, pretending he was tying his shoes. Catching the Sun Devils off guard, Mike flipped the ball to Gary Allen, who dashed for a quick 28-yard run.

In the fourth quarter, we ran the play again, only with a twist: Mike Stennis again flipped the ball to Gary. This time, however, Gary handed the ball off on a reverse to DeWayne Jett, who sprinted to the right side of the line of scrimmage. With a couple of Sun Devils bearing down on him, DeWayne leaped into the air and threw a 40-yard pass into the waiting arms of Stennis.

It was one of the most memorable plays in my time at UH.

I mean, DeWayne threw a jump pass. I had never seen anyone do that before.

DeWayne Jett (UH WR, 1976-79): *Okay, here's the true and honest reason for the jump pass: As I got the ball on the run, I knew ASU had seen the reverse. I didn't want to stop to set up to throw the ball. If I stopped, anyone pursuing me might have gotten to me before I could get the pass off. Being a one-time quarterback, I knew I could throw the ball on the run. So I jumped and threw a tight spiral right over Mike's shoulder. People say I did it for dramatic effect, but the truth is I didn't want to get sacked!*

Believe it or not, DeWayne's 40-yard pass would be our only completed pass of the game. No matter. Final score: Hawaiʻi 29, Arizona State 17. Not only did we secure our second straight winning season, but we did it in dominating fashion. Attendance that night was 42,040, giving us a record season turnout of 334,364.

I have one more vivid memory of our victory over ASU. As the game was winding down, I turned to Jesse Sapolu, who was then a wide-eyed freshman. I said, "Jesse, you could be over there [with ASU]." The Sun Devils had heavily recruited Jesse, but ultimately he chose to play for us.

"Well, Coach," he said, smiling, "I'm glad I'm not."

Jesse Sapolu: *I played both ways against Colorado State and Arizona State. I was even able to record a quarterback sack. That was my highlight as a defensive player!*

The next year, in 1980, we hosted West Virginia, which was led by quarterback Oliver Luck (the father of current NFL star Andrew Luck). The real story behind this game, however, was what happened one week earlier.

We opened the 1980 season with victories over Abilene Christian and Pacific. In our third game, however, we were beaten badly by Wyoming in Laramie. We returned to Honolulu looking for redemption. Instead, we got whipped by an average UTEP team, 34-14, in front of 40,421 disappointed fans.

We had laid a big fat egg.

It was as poor of a performance as I've ever been a part of, and I was steamed. The next few days, we made the guys sit in the room and watch the game film over and over and over and over again. We sat there for a long time and just stewed in our own juices. We knew what a dreadful effort the UTEP game was. Everybody got called out, including the head coach. I remember telling the team that if we expected to produce a similar effort against West Virginia and expect to beat them, we were out of our freaking minds.

Larry Goeas: *When we lost to UTEP, we were at a crisis point. We had started the season as one of the favorites to win the WAC, but we'd just lost two conference games in a row. Dick knew that we had to shake things up.*

We usually watched game film in our media rooms, with our offense and defense meeting separately. But not this time. Instead, we all met at Campus Center and watched the UTEP loss as a team. There was a lot of screaming and yelling. Coach kept showing the same plays over and over, screaming, "Look at this! Look at this!"

Then Dick said, "Guys, we're not going home. We're going to go down to the field and run sprints. We did sixteen 110-yard sprints. We were gassed. Then he said, "You know what? We need to do eight more."

Believe me, the next day the tone of our practice changed. It was rough and physical. Thursdays were usually a light workout with shoulder pads, but that week we had a full workout. Looking back on it, this was a real turning point for us.

Despite our loss to UTEP, 41,889 fans showed up to Aloha Stadium to cheer us on against West Virginia. They were treated to quite a game.

The Mountaineers, who came into the game 4-1, struck early with a pair of field goals. Our offense was struggling and failed to put up a single point until early in the fourth quarter, when senior fullback George Bell rumbled into the end zone for a 2-yard score. Gary Allen followed that up with a 1-yard score of his own.

West Virginia, meanwhile, was relying heavily on their star running back, Robert Alexander, who was known as "Alexander the Great." Alexander finished with 152 rushing yards, but we kept him out of the end zone.

Mark Kafentzis (UH DB, 1980-81): *I knocked Oliver Luck out of the game. It was funny because we both later ended up with the Houston Oilers. He was the backup to Warren Moon. He kind of put two and two together and figured out who I was. He reminded me of that play!*

With less than two minutes in the contest, the score was tied at 13 apiece.

Niko Noga stuffs a Nebraska lineman n the 1982 season finale.

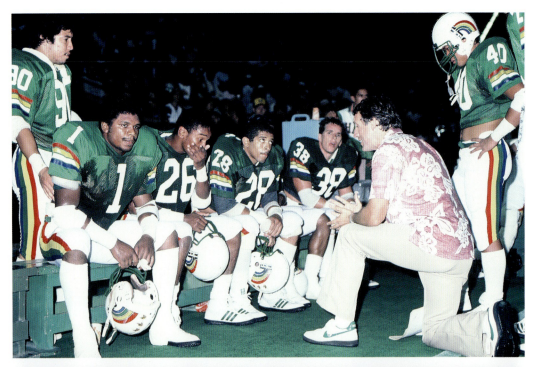

Top: Bob Wagner coaches up defensive backs Vernon Gearing, Brian Norwood, Marty Sims and Rich Miano. **Above:** The 1981 Rainbow Warriors, who won 11 straight games over two seasons, were the first ranked team in UH football history.

Top: Tim Lyons checks his receivers downfield against BYU in 1981. **Above:** In the same game, linebacker Anthony Woodson squares off against Cougar quarterback Jim McMahon.

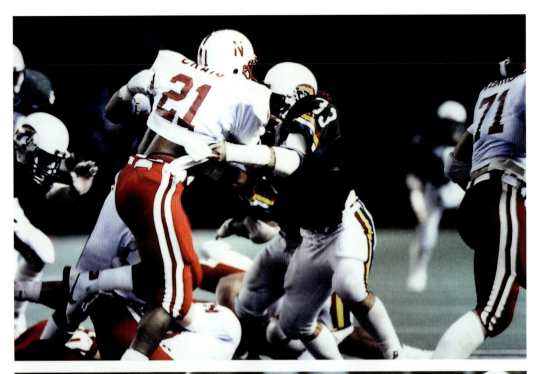

Steve Lehor stops Nebraska running back Roger Craig (top) while (below) the defense causes a turnover in the 1982 finale against Nebraska, which Hawaiʻi led 16-7 going into the fourth quarter.

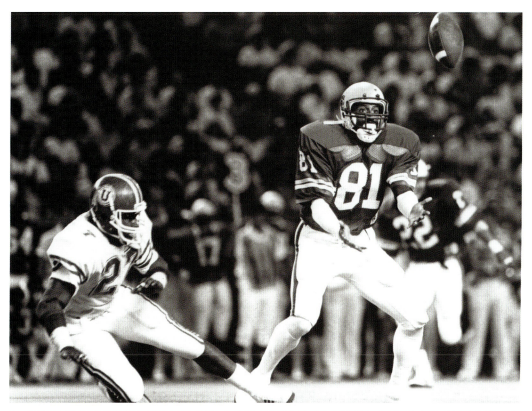

Top: Walter Murray beats a Utah safety to the ball. **Above:** The high-energy UH cheerleaders before a packed house in 1981.

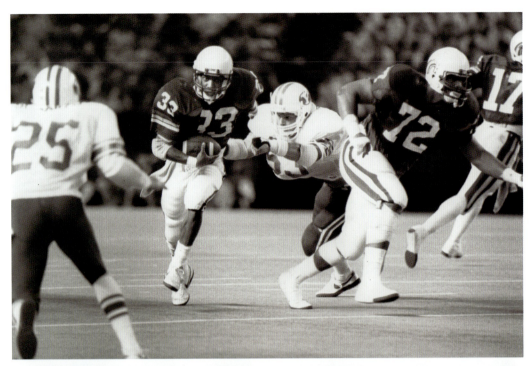

Top: Marco Johnson runs the ball against BYU in 1984. **Above:** On the sidelines, Coach Tomey makes his point to Rich Miano.

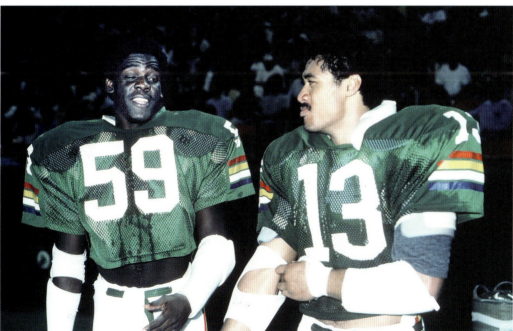

Top: With his signature flattop, Na Koa Football Club co-founder Ben Yee was a regular fixture at Rainbow Warriors games. **Above:** Linebackers M.L. Johnson and Alvis Satele.

Mike Gibson and Jim Asmus hoist Coach Tomey after the emotional victory over West Virginia in 1980.

Earlier in the game, our kicker, Jim Asmus, missed both a field goal and an extra point. Those were his first miscues of the season, and he was dying for a chance to redeem himself.

He got that chance late in the fourth quarter, when linebacker Doug Kyle nailed Alexander after a screen pass. Doug jarred the ball loose and Mark Kafentzis recovered at the Mountaineer 32.

Nineteen seconds before the final gun, Jim calmly booted a 40-yard kick through the uprights, giving us a 16-13 lead.

Jim Asmus (UH PK/P, 1979-80): *The West Virginia game has to be one of my favorites, for sure. It was a great win for us. I was so happy because I didn't think I performed very well in that game. It was the first time I missed a field goal all year. To be able to come back and redeem myself, that was a neat feeling.*

The Mountaineers had one final gasp, and they set up for a 50-yard field goal attempt with the seconds ticking away. WVU's Steve Sinclair wound up for the game-tying kick.

The kick was blocked! Time expired, and a bunch of happy Rainbow Warriors rushed the field!

The guy who made the block was a young freshman defensive lineman out of Farrington High School. His name? Falaniko Noga.

Falaniko Noga: *I blocked the field goal with just seconds left in the game. The first person to run out and tackle me was Coach Tomey! I didn't believe it at first, but later on I watched the game film. Sure enough, he was the first guy in on the celebration.*

One side note to the West Virginia game: It was the first game that Jesse Sapolu played center for us. Our starting center, senior Ed Riewerts, was out for the game with an injury. We needed someone to fill in, and Jesse did a great job. In fact, he was named the game's outstanding lineman.

Jesse Sapolu: *I had never played center before. Taking a step back and snapping your hand back were totally new to me. I remember staying after practice that week to make sure I didn't fumble the snaps. I was out there on the practice field until seven o'clock at night. We used the lights from the baseball stadium to help us see. Really, I was thrown into the fire against one of the top football programs in the country.*

Jesse, of course, would later become an All-Pro center for the San Francisco 49ers, helping the Niners to four Super Bowl championships.

Larry Goeas: *To me, the West Virginia game was so memorable because of the struggles we had gone through earlier in the season. The thing is, the win convinced Dick that this was the way we needed to practice all the time. He said, "I've got it figured out. We got to really work you guys."*

Our history-making 1981 team closed its season against South Carolina, a school we had beaten in my first season in Hawai'i. This time around, Gamecocks head coach Jim Carlen didn't make any condescending remarks before the game. Our 24-7 victory over his team in 1977 ensured that he would not overlook us again.

It didn't matter. We won again, 33-10, even though two of our best players, Gary Allen and Dana McLemore, sat out the finale with injuries.

Everybody got into the act in this victory. David Toloumu, in his final game as a Rainbow Warrior, got things going with a 10-yard touchdown reception from Bernard Quarles. In the second quarter, Tim Lyons tossed a 6-yard touchdown pass to Merv Lopes. Second-half scores by Ron Pennick and Anthony Edgar sealed the game for us.

This was no upset. We were simply the better team. The 1981 team started the season a perfect 7-0, and, dating back to the previous year, won eleven straight games. In our first seven games, we outscored our opponents by a combined score of 216 to 78!

In early November, we earned a national ranking for the first time in our program's history, coming in at No. 16. Then came a couple of demoralizing losses: a 13-3 heartbreaker to BYU that ended our WAC championship hopes, and a 23-17 upset at the hands of Pacific. We got back on the track the following week, pounding Colorado State by 53 points.

Beating the Gamecocks allowed us to finish the season at 9-2, the most wins at UH since Dave Holmes' 1973 team.

The most notable aspect of this game was bidding aloha to our stellar senior class, which included Gary Allen, Keith Ah Yuen, Dana McLemore, David Toloumu, Marcus Tarver, Andy Moody, Larry Goeas, Tony Holyfield, Kani Kauahi, Merv Lopes, Ron Pennick, Verlon Redd, Semeri Ulufale, Reggie Robinson, Noland Baker and Dave Barbour.

There's one more thing I'd like to add about our 1981 team: We had a tremendous offensive line. We had Keith Ah Yuen and Jesse Sapolu on the left side, Kani Kauahi at center, and Jim Donovan and Jim Mills lined up on the right. Bernard Carvalho and Noland Baker also saw extensive playing time. Their position coach was Ed Kezirian, who was as good a coach as I've ever worked with.

Not many people know this, but when Ed joined our program from UCLA for the 1978 season, my buddy Terry Donahue still kept a close eye on him. In fact, for three straight seasons, Terry offered Ed a job on the Bruins' staff. And in each of those seasons, Ed turned down the opportunity.

He told me, "I don't want to even want to think about leaving until I feel like I've done the job that I was hired to do." It was a rare display of loyalty and commitment to his first full-time coaching assignment. Only at the end of the 1981 season did Ed feel ready to move on and return to UCLA.

We replaced Ed with Mike Hill, who also did a tremendous job for us. In fact, we were exceptionally blessed at this staff position, as Ed Riewerts and Bill Souza would later succeed Mike. Good offensive line coaches are hard to find.

The Nebraska Cornhuskers were our opponents for our 1982 season finale. Tom Osborne's team had given us a beatdown in 1978, but now we were far better prepared and equipped to face this perennial national power.

The 1982 Cornhuskers were better than their 1978 counterparts as well. They arrived at Aloha Stadium with a roster loaded with future NFL stars, including running backs Mike Rozier and Roger Craig, wide receiver Irving Fryar, and offensive linemen Dave Rimington and Dean Steinkuhler. Rozier would go on to win the 1983 Heisman Trophy. Craig would win three Super Bowl rings with the San Francisco 49ers. Fryar was the NFL's No. 1 draft pick in 1984. And Rimington and Steinkuhler combined to win three Outland Trophies and two Lombardi Awards. It's no wonder the odds-makers had us as 28-point underdogs.

We struck first, with senior quarterback Bernard Quarles scoring on a 4-yard run in the first quarter. In the second quarter, Lee Larsen added a 40-yard field goal to put us ahead, 10-0, at halftime.

That's right. We had shut down Nebraska's vaunted offensive attack in the first half. Our defense forced three turnovers, including a jarring hit and fumble recovery by linebacker Anthony Woodson. We even surprised the Huskers with a second-quarter onside kick.

We added another field goal at the start of the second half. Fryar got Nebraska on the board with a terrific 31-yard run, but we followed that up with another field goal.

As the clock wound down on the third quarter, we were leading Nebraska, 16-7. *Honolulu Advertiser* writer Andy Yamaguchi, anticipating a historic Rainbow Warrior victory, called his office with possible headlines.

"How's this for a headline?" he said. "Green Giants Can Cornhuskers!"

Unfortunately, the fourth quarter—all of it—belonged to Nebraska and their gutsy quarterback, Turner Gill. We ended up losing the game, 37-16.

Dino Babers (UH RB/LB/S, 1979-83): *Turner Gill had a hurt shoulder, so he didn't play in the first half. When Nebraska came out in the second half, he still didn't have his pads on. So now we're about halfway through the third quarter and we're still winning. All of a sudden, Turner Gill takes off his jersey and puts* *his shoulder pads on. Everybody in the stadium erupted. I thought, "What in the hell is going on?"*

Turner entered the game, and everyone got excited. We thought, "We're going to beat Nebraska with Turner Gill!"

The first time he touched the ball, Turner handed it off to Roger Craig, and we blew up the play for no gain. The whole place was going crazy! But after that, Irving Fryar scored on a long run. Then Turner scored on an 18-yard run. Craig followed that with another score. Finally, Fryar scored again, this time on a 70-yard punt return.

The next thing I know, Turner Gill's taking off his pads on the sideline and the game was over.

We closed the 1983 season with another top-ranked team, the Oklahoma Sooners. Again, we were 28-point underdogs. And, again, we gave the heavy favorite all they could handle.

More than 45,000 fans showed up at Aloha Stadium to see us host Barry Switzer's Sooners, who were led by running back Spencer Tillman.

A Hawai'i fan caught our attention before the start of the game. He claimed that he had inside information that Oklahoma was going to run a reverse to receiver George "Buster" Rhymes on the first play of the game. He even drew the play up for us in the parking lot. Of course, we had no way of knowing whether the tip was legitimate or not. When the game began, we told our defense to be alert just in case the Sooners ran the reverse.

Sure enough, on the very first play, they ran the damn reverse for a bunch of yards. Our linebacker, Mike Beazley, was in position to make the stop, but the guy who demonstrated the play for us in the parking lot was not Buster Rhymes.

Before the season, we brought in an aspiring young coach that you may have heard of—June Jones. June was somebody I got to know through his good friend, former UH basketball player Artie Wilson. June, who had played quarterback at UH in 1974, was interested in returning to the Islands as a full-time coach for us.

I could see right away that June had tremendous potential. The sky was the limit for him. At the same time, however, it was clear that he really wanted to coach in the NFL. His one season as our quarterbacks coach would be a good steppingstone for June.

As you might guess, with June on board, this edition of the Rainbow Warriors emphasized the passing game a lot more. The Oklahoma game exemplified that. Our quarterback, Raphel Cherry (also called Ralph), threw the ball 34 times for 261 yards. His favorite receiver, Walter Murray, was even more outstanding, pulling in 10 receptions for 201 yards and a pair of touchdowns.

Walter Murray: *My biggest game as a Rainbow Warrior was against the Sooners. That season, we were passing the ball like crazy, which made me happy. Before the game, I remember being at the team hotel and Raphel Cherry stole my clothes! I don't know if he was just messing with me or if he thought I was too nervous—and I was very nervous before this game—but he just swiped my clothes.*

So instead of stressing out about the game, all of a sudden I'm running around the hotel trying to find my clothes. Finally, one of the coaches tells me, "Go to Ralph's room. He has your stuff." So I go to his room, grab my clothes and call him a couple of names I can't repeat. But it worked out because it took away my nervousness."

Midway through the second quarter, David Aguilar, a redshirt freshman receiver out of Punahou, blocked a Sooners punt to set up our first touchdown. (David later changed his surname to "Dyas.") Raphel hooked up with Walter Murray for a 46-yard score. Later, with just twenty seconds left before intermission, Kerry Brady kicked a 42-yard field goal to add to our lead. It was Kerry's first field goal attempt for us all season. Our starting kicker, Richard Spelman, had been knocked out of the game after the first kickoff.

Unbelievably, just like the Nebraska game the year before, we led the Sooners, 10-0, at halftime.

Brian Derby: *We didn't care if it was Oklahoma or Iowa or Nebraska. Our thing was, "When you guys come here to play us, we're going to kick your ass." That was our mindset. We had no fear.*

I know Coach Tomey thought we were mentally "out there," especially me and [offensive lineman] Quentin Flores. They thought we were mentally unstable. Quentin's nickname was Mad Dog. He was always barking like a dog.

We'd come up to the line and say, "The ball's coming right here." Our opponents would think we were just trying to mess with them, but we'd run the ball exactly where we said we'd run it. They'd tell us, "You guys are crazy, telling us where the ball's going to be run?" And we'd say, "Yeah. Try and stop it!"

Unfortunately, again, we couldn't keep the lead. The Sooner defense, led by their great senior safety, Scott Case, kept our offense in check in the second half. Another Cherry-Murray TD connection put us ahead, 17-14, in the fourth quarter, but that was it. Sooner quarterback Danny Bradley's 2-yard touchdown with 6:57 left in the fourth put Oklahoma ahead for good. Final score: Oklahoma 21, Hawaiʻi 17.

The Sooners' defensive backs coach, Bobby Proctor, couldn't stop marveling about Ralph and Walter. "Cherry was as good as we've seen throwing the ball," he said. "And that damn 81 [meaning Walter] is just so good. Coming into the game, I thought Murray was the second-best receiver we would face after [Nebraska's]

Irving Fryar. Now I think he's on a par."

Brian Derby: *What an incredible athlete Ralph Cherry was. With June Jones as our quarterback coach, he put up some ridiculous numbers.*

I was his center at the time, and his locker was next to mine. He would always say, "Damn, Derb, wash your damn pants!" I never liked to wash my pants because I hated to put my pads in all the time. My classes finished late, and I just wanted to get to my locker, put my stuff on, get taped and go. So I'd leave my pants dirty for a few days.

"I have to put my hands on you, and your pants stink," Ralph would complain. Then I'd say, "Well, put your hand there and just don't think about it. Or put some Vicks under your nose!"

Finally, Ralph would tell me, "I'll tell you what. If I take you to Burger King, will you wash your pants?" And you know us offensive linemen can be bought, right?

When I heard what happened with Ralph, I was, like, "Oh, man." It's too bad what happened to him.

While writing this book, I went back and forth on how I should handle the subject of Raphel Cherry. It's an extremely sensitive situation, and to be honest it's something I'm not very comfortable talking about.

Ralph was a terrific quarterback who could do it all. Standing six feet tall and weighing a solid 200 pounds, Ralph could run and throw. Without a doubt, he would have been outstanding in the run-and-shoot offenses that many college football programs employ today. In our 1983 season, under the tutelage of June Jones, Ralph set twenty-two UH passing and total offense records. He later played safety in the NFL for the Washington Redskins and Detroit Lions.

Ralph was responsible for the best play I've ever seen a quarterback make that wasn't a run or a pass. We were in a tight game against Utah in 1982, and the game was tied in the fourth quarter, 7-7. The Utes had a great defensive end named Filipo Mokofisi, who would later earn WAC Defensive Player of the Year honors.

Ralph dropped back to pass, and just as he was ready to launch one of his patented "Cherry Bombs," he instinctively felt Mokofisi coming at him. Right before he got hit, Ralph somehow managed to tuck the ball and secure it to his chest. Believe me, Mokofisi hit him like a runaway train, and the ball should have popped out. But thanks to Ralph, we kept possession and went on to win the game with a last-second field goal. It was an amazing play that showed unselfishness, toughness and great instinct.

But here's the sad and troubling fact: In 1999, Ralph was convicted in the strangulation death of his wife, Jerri. He was originally sentenced to life in prison, but a subsequent appeal reduced the penalty to thirty years. He'll be eligible for parole in 2020.

Obviously, it's a sad and awful situation. It was a horrendous crime. What happened? How did it all go wrong? I don't know.

Several of his former coaches and teammates, myself included, have tried to reach out to Ralph. So far, he hasn't responded. We want him to know that we are there for him, and that we have not given up on Raphel Cherry.

The Ralph that I knew was not a murderer, yet the facts speak for themselves. Right now, he is serving time in an Arkansas penitentiary. My hope is that, if and when he is released from prison, he will be able to somehow put his life back together and find peace. It won't be easy.

Joe Onosai (UH OL, 1983-86): *I've done a lot of ministry work in prisons, and I've personally mentored individuals who spent a lot of years in prison. I believe that there is redemption. If Raphel Cherry is given that opportunity, I think he can find redemption. I believe in redemption. He'll need to hang out with the right people and find mentors who can help him and build him up.*

When we found out about what happened, we were all shocked. And we were disappointed because it was so uncharacteristic of the man we knew him to be. The Ralph that I knew was such a gentleman.

Hopefully, he will be able to move on from this, give back to the community and enjoy the rest of his life. He's going to face a lot of challenges; for example, it's going to be hard for him to get a job. But if he can find a support team and some sort of structure to help him transition back into the community, he'll be okay.

The next season, on December 2, 1984, we closed with the Iowa Hawkeyes. After an 0-3 start to the season, we had won seven straight games. Upsetting Hayden Fry's Hawkeyes would be the perfect way to cap a remarkable year.

Iowa was led by junior quarterback Chuck Long, who would later play six NFL seasons and be inducted into the College Football Hall of Fame. Long would be locked in a passing duel with senior Raphel Cherry, who was playing his final game as a Rainbow Warrior.

We led 6-3 at the half, thanks to a pair of Richard Spelman field goals. Coach Fry later told *The Honolulu Advertiser*, "At halftime, I told the team that we're a lot closer to Hawai'i than Oklahoma and Nebraska had been."

The score remained 6-3 as the fourth quarter began. Our defense had made an impressive stand just a few minutes earlier, sending the 50,000 fans in attendance into a frenzy. On first down, defensive tackle Colin Scotts broke in from the left side and hit Long as he threw, forcing an incomplete pass. On the next play, Al Noga stopped Iowa running back Fred Bush at the line of scrimmage. Then, on third down, senior linebacker Alvis Satele dropped Long for an 8-yard loss.

It felt like the stadium was going to explode.

Our offense got the ball on our own 34-yard line. On the first play, Ralph hit senior receiver Joe Nobles for a big 24-yard gain. On the next snap, however, Ralph coughed up the football and Iowa recovered.

Long engineered two touchdown drives in that decisive fourth quarter, and we ended up falling to the Hawkeyes, 17-6.

In 1986, we played a rare early-season home game against a powerhouse opponent: the Wisconsin Badgers of the Big Ten Conference. We had just come off a season-opening road loss to Air Force, and we were hungry for a chance to get a big W.

It didn't look good for us early on. Badger cornerback Nate Odomes returned an interception 73 yards for the first score of the game. Odomes was spectacular in this game, snaring three picks in all.

Wisconsin led, 17-3, in the third quarter. Rod Valverde's second field goal of the night drew us closer, 17-6. And that's when our quarterback, Gregg Tipton, went to work.

Gregg had a poor showing against Air Force, and he certainly didn't start well against the Badgers. But late in the fourth quarter, he was razor sharp: Gregg threw a 10-yard pass to our running back Danny Crowell. Then he fired a 24-yard strike to running back Marco Johnson. That was followed by a 19-yard throw to David Dyas. Finally, with 3:27 to play, Gregg found tight end Ron Hall in the end zone. Rod's extra point made it 17-13, Wisconsin.

Our defense, led by Al Noga and linebackers Thad Jefferson and M.J. Johnson, stonewalled the Badgers on their next possession, and we got the ball again.

Again, Gregg led us down the field. He fired a 25-yard pass over the middle to David Dyas, who made a leaping catch and fell on Wisconsin's 18-yard line. One play later, Gregg and David connected again, with David beating Odomes before getting pushed out at the 2-yard line.

You know what? I'm not going to describe what happened next. Instead, here's the play-by-play call by the great Jim Leahey, who announced the game on KHNL that night with his broadcast partner, Rick Blangiardi. Here's Jim:

> "The clock is running! Thirty-nine…thirty-eight…thirty-seven! The ball is inside the two on the near hash mark. Thirty-three…thirty-two…thirty-one! The Rainbows break the huddle. They come to the line. I-formation. Crowell and [Walter] Briggs. Tipton gives it to Briggs…LEAPS! Doesn't get it! Doesn't get it!"
>
> "Nineteen seconds left! Rainbows call a timeout! They have the ball inside the Wisconsin 1! The Rainbows, who have spent the night in frustration, who have spent the night trying and trying again, now have a chance to win it! Nineteen seconds left! This is storybook! This is what Division I college football is all about! Out of the huddle come the Rainbows. You see the story right there. I-formation behind Tipton. Second and goal to go. Tipton turns, gives it…no, he has it! He's

going to dive for the end zone! Does he get it? YES! TOUCHDOWN!"

What a memorable call on a memorable play. And just seconds later, Rick Blangiardi began screaming, *"There are no flags! No flags! The touchdown is good!"*

Hawai'i 20, Wisconsin 17. What a game!

Later in 1986, we closed our season by hosting another Big Ten power: the Michigan Wolverines and their coach—and my dearest mentor—Bo Schembechler.

The Wolverines had just beaten their biggest rival, Ohio State, in a 26-24 thriller. Their quarterback was Jim Harbaugh, who is now the school's head coach.

Michigan had a monster of an offensive tackle in 307-pound John "Jumbo" Elliott. However, we had Al Noga. Everyone was anticipating a titanic clash between the two All-Americans, and the battle more than lived up to the hype.

"He's definitely an All-American," a weary Elliott said of Al after the game.

Al more than held his own against Elliott and his fellow lineman. He remarked after the game, "Size don't mean shit. You gotta have heart. If you don't have heart, I'm gonna punch you in the face on that football field." Al finished the game with nine tackles, two for a loss.

Once again, the Rainbow Warriors rose to the occasion against one of college football's premier teams. We battled the Wolverines to a 3-3 tie heading into halftime. Harbaugh scored on a 4-yard quarterback keeper early in the third, but again we responded. Coyle Permetter, a sophomore fullback from Anchorage, Alaska, bulled his way into the end zone to knot the game at 10.

In the fourth quarter, the game simply got away from us. Harbaugh engineered a pair of touchdown drives, and Michigan added a field goal to win, 27-10.

I was so proud of our team. We lost, but we put up an effort that was second to none.

"That's the best we've ever played in a game," I told the *Advertiser*'s Ferd Lewis. "Much better than Oklahoma, Nebraska or any of those other teams. And this is the best team we've ever done it against."

Then I nodded toward the Michigan locker room and added, "I think those guys know they were in a damn football game."

After the game, Bo came to our locker room and addressed our team. He said he was proud of our guys and complimented us on the way we played. It was just a wonderful moment that I will never forget. What a huge honor it was for us. Bo was never the type to do something just for show. I admired Bo so much. For him to take the time to talk to us like that, I don't remember a greater honor ever in all my years of coaching.

Chapter Six

THE ONE THAT GOT AWAY

September 22, 1984. The final gun had sounded, and most of the 50,000 fans at Aloha Stadium were slowly, dejectedly making their way to the exits. The adrenaline-filled thrill ride that had rocked Hālawa throughout this autumn night had given way to a much more somber mood. A smattering of people remained in the stands, arms crossed, eyes glazed.

It was like surveying the aftermath of a major disaster.

I stood on the field near the south end zone, not quite sure what to do. All around me, Rainbow Warrior players and coaches and trainers and equipment managers were struggling to find the right words—*any* words—to console each other.

We had just lost a heartbreaking game to our biggest rival. We gave everything we had in that contest, but came up short. The scoreboard said it all: BYU 18, Hawai'i 13.

Moments later, I walked into our locker room. There was dead silence. I looked around and saw all the guys in tears. They were devastated. They were broken.

For the first time in my coaching career, I didn't know what to say.

In my ten years as head football coach at the University of Hawai'i, we were able to catalog some great accomplishments: We joined the Western Athletic Conference. We set home attendance records. We beat collegiate powerhouses such as South Carolina (twice), Arizona State, West Virginia and Wisconsin. We achieved the program's first-ever national ranking and had our games shown on national television.

The one thing we couldn't do?

We couldn't beat BYU.

Oh, we came close. Some of our games, in fact, were *excruciatingly* close. But we could never get the job done.

Make no mistake, we wanted to beat the Cougars. Our fans wanted to see us beat the Cougars. With every loss to Lavell Edwards and his team, that desire to vanquish BYU just continued to grow.

The rivalry extended beyond football. Our university's baseball team counted the Cougars as a bitter adversary. So did our women's volleyball team. In 1989, after our men's basketball team snapped an eleven-game losing streak against BYU, a jubilant David Hallums danced on the court and shouted, "This is better than statehood!"

Beating BYU meant that much.

Joe Onosai: *Because I grew up in Hawai'i, I always cheered for Hawai'i to beat BYU. We could never beat them, and I think that's what made the rivalry even more special for us. They were the gold standard in the Western Athletic Conference, and we would always be disappointed when we lost to them.*

It's ironic because Coach Tomey would always preach to us about winning the game in the fourth quarter. We were usually able to do just that. But against BYU, for whatever reason, we always found ways to lose in the final quarter. But even then, it just gave us a bigger desire to beat them. And it wasn't just us. All of our fans felt the same way.

Walter Murray: *Oh, man. BYU was the only team we could never beat the whole time I was at UH. It got to the point where I couldn't stand them. I even hated Danny Ainge, and he didn't even play football! I didn't like Steve Young, either, but we both ended up with the San Francisco 49ers and I got to know him pretty well.*

I used to get upset because I thought that BYU cheated. I mean, a player goes to BYU and redshirts his first year. And then, if he's still not ready, he goes on a two-year mission. He comes back bigger and stronger, and he's twenty-five years old! I don't know if that's really what was happening, but that's what it seemed like at the time.

The first Hawai'i-BYU football game was held way back in 1930. UH trounced the Cougars, 49-13. Of course, that was a lifetime ago. Until I arrived in the Islands, the most recent matchup had happened in 1974. The Rainbow Warriors beat BYU, 15-13, thanks to five field goals by placekicker Reinhold Stuprich.

We played the Cougars again in 1978, my second season in Hawai'i. We raced out to a 13-0 lead in the first quarter, but BYU quarterback Marc Wilson dominated the rest of the way. Wilson passed for 291 yards and a pair of touchdowns. He also scrambled for a team-high 61 yards.

For Hawai'i fans, the lone highlight of the game was the play of freshman tailback Gary Allen. Gary scored our first touchdown on a magnificent 75-yard open-field run. He would finish with 138 yards on 21 carries, breaking the school record for most rushing yards in a season by a freshman.

The honest truth is, we weren't ready physically to compete with the Cougars. We were able to make some good plays here and there, but they were just a more mature program than we were at that time. BYU also had the benefit of having tremendous continuity on the coaching staff, led, of course, by the great Lavell Edwards. (For you trivia buffs: One of their assistant coaches was Fred Whittingham. Fred was the father of Kyle Whittingham, who is now the head coach at Utah.)

How did the rivalry start? Well, at the time, BYU dominated the Western Athletic Conference, the league that we joined in 1979. They were the best the WAC had to offer, and of course that made them a natural target. If you like baseball and you're in the American League East Division, you don't like the New York Yankees because they're usually the team to beat. The presence of BYU-Hawaiʻi and the Mormon church on Oʻahu also made the Cougars a natural rival. That meant that we were adversaries on the recruiting front as well, as Coach Edwards and his staff did their best to poach local talent from our state.

We played BYU again in 1979, this time in Provo, Utah. Then, in 1980, we hosted the Cougars at Aloha Stadium in front of 49,139 fans—our largest home crowd to date. In both games, we again lost by lopsided scores. The 1980 loss was memorable because of the performance of BYU quarterback Jim McMahon. The future Super Bowl-winning signal caller threw sixty passes in that game (a national record at the time). Even more remarkable was the huge play that he made that just crushed our spirits. McMahon, who doubled as the Cougars' punter, had a snap sail high over his head. He somehow managed to retrieve the ball. As our defenders were bearing down on him, he turned to his left, took a couple of steps and kicked the ball with his left foot. *His left foot.*

The ball hit the turf and began rolling toward the end zone. It seemed like it rolled forever. But it finally stopped. On the 1-yard line.

That was Jim McMahon. He simply found ways to make positive things happen.

> **Jim Asmus:** *I remember that game. We just weren't playing well. Coach Tomey was livid at halftime. Right before we took the field for the second half, he turned to me in frustration and said, "Jim, I'm so sick and tired of everyone telling me how good you are. Just kick the damn ball!"*
>
> *Then he turned around and kicked a trash can, not realizing that it was full. As we left the locker room, our trainer Eric Okazaki had to tape up his foot. That was pretty funny, but I didn't dare laugh!"*

Our 1981 game was a different story. Our team had the talent and experience to finally beat the Cougars. We were 7-0 coming into the game, and we had an eleven-game winning streak dating back to the previous season. Even better, we had cracked the national polls for the first time in program history. We were ranked No. 16, just one spot ahead of the Cougars.

Jesse Sapolu: *After learning about our ranking, I remembered the words of Coach Tomey when he was recruiting me. He said, "Do you want to be a part of a program that's already established, or do you want to be a part of a group that brings your hometown team to prominence?" It was an incredible feeling. All of us were walking around campus, giggling. We couldn't believe it.*

The game was held on November 14, 1981 at Aloha Stadium. It was an afternoon game because, for the first time in UH history, our game would be broadcast on national TV (ABC Sports). More importantly, the winner of this game would have the inside track on the WAC title. (Remember, this was before the football conferences had league championship games.)

This was the final opportunity for our great 1978 recruiting class to win a conference championship. Gary Allen, David Toloumu, Dana McLemore, Marcus Tarver, Andy Moody and the rest of our seniors were raring to go!

The game started with a pair of textbook tackles by Dana. Our defense stopped the Cougars cold, and the Aloha Stadium crowd of 45,355 roared their approval.

Dana McLemore (UH defensive back/punt returner, 1978-81): *I knew that if I could cover those BYU receivers, I could do pretty good in the NFL. Man, we played BYU every year, and they always had really good quarterbacks. I remember one of our coaches telling us, "Don't hurt Jim McMahon. His backup is even better than he is." That was Steve Young.*

Unfortunately, BYU's defense was just as good, if not better. It was apparent early on that the two teams would be locked in a defensive battle.

After a scoreless first quarter, the Cougars got on the board with a 19-yard field goal. Another BYU field goal, this time from 45 yards out, made it 6-0 at the half. We started to move the ball in the third quarter. Bernard Quarles, who shared quarterback duties with Tim Lyons in this contest, connected on a 42-yard pass play to fellow UCLA transfer Anthony Edgar. That big gain set up a 40-yard field goal by our barefooted placekicker, Lee Larsen.

The play of the game occurred late in the third. Led by Jim McMahon, the Cougars were marching down the field. Then McMahon threw a pass to running back Waymon Hamilton, who fumbled the ball on the 5-yard line. Players on both teams dived for the ball, and it bounced into the end zone and into the waiting arms of BYU flanker Neil Balholm.

It would be the only touchdown by either team. BYU prevailed, 13-3.

Rich Miano (UH safety, 1981-84): *You know the cliché: "It only counts as one game," or "You take it one game at a time." But deep down, you know how beating BYU was. It was by far the biggest rivalry in UH history, maybe even the entire state. I know the fans wanted a win, but nobody left Aloha Stadium feeling like we weren't the aggressor or the tougher team. We left everything on the field.* (Note: Rich did not play in that 1981 game, as he sat out the season as a redshirt.)

Larry Goeas: *It was the only time in my life that I cried after a game. We really wanted to beat those guys.*

Today, that fumble recovery in the end zone wouldn't be a touchdown. Current rules state that you can't advance the ball by bobbling it forward.

It was a tough way to lose, but I was proud of the way we hung tough from opening kickoff to the game's final play. We were only the second team that season to hold McMahon without a touchdown.

The Cougars' defense was even more impressive. Our star tailback, Gary Allen, was held to minus-1 rushing yards. Anthony Edgar, his talented backup, could only muster 17 yards.

"Hawai'i played tough defense," McMahon said after the game. "But ours played better. It was a battle of defenses, and ours won."

That loss hurt us emotionally. The next week, we played horribly and fell to Pacific at home. I take responsibility for that. I didn't understand how critical it was to give our guys a chance to recover from the BYU game.

We were still nationally ranked after losing to BYU. After the loss to Pacific, however, we pretty much dropped off the map.

Things didn't get any easier for us the next season, in 1982. McMahon was now with the NFL's Chicago Bears, but the Cougars simply rolled out another All-American quarterback.

In many ways, Steve Young was just like McMahon. In fact, I'd say that the two were more similar than they were different. Both were excellent runners. Both could throw the ball. And both became great NFL talents. If anything, I think Young was a more polished signal caller. Jim, on the other hand, wasn't necessarily a pretty quarterback. But he was a fabulous competitor and a really tough guy. Sometimes I think he willed his teams to wins.

The 1982 game was held in Provo. Cougar Stadium had just expanded to accommodate 65,000 fans, and on that day every seat was filled. We came into the game with a solid 4-1 record, losing only to Wyoming in our fourth game of the season.

We were expecting more aerial fireworks from BYU. Instead, we found out that the Cougars were just as dangerous running the ball.

We struck first, with Bernard Quarles connecting with Walter Murray for a picture-perfect 32-yard score. Later in the opening quarter, Bernard threw a strike to Anthony Edgar for a 53-yard touchdown. In the second quarter, Bernard kept the ball and ran it into the end zone for a 21-yard score. On the down side, we missed the extra point after all three of those touchdowns. BYU led, 19-18, at halftime.

In the end, BYU won this game because of their offensive line. While our quarterbacks (Bernard Quarles and Raphel Cherry) were sacked four times, our defense couldn't get to Steve Young. Our standout linebacker, Carl Kenneybrew, remarked after the game: "There was nothing fancy about what they did. They were more physical and got the job done. They had the power to do what they wanted, and they did it."

Leading 32-25, BYU had the ball with about six or seven minutes left in the game. We needed to stop them to have a chance to score a game-tying touchdown. Instead, we watched helplessly from the sidelines as the Cougars just ran the ball down our throats.

We had tried to recruit running back Casey Tiumalu, but he'd signed with BYU. On this day, Tiumalu hitched the Cougars' offense on his back and marched down the field. We needed to stop the run and force them to throw. But that didn't happen.

BYU ran the same draw play seven times in a row, with Tiumalu finishing the drive with a game-clinching 21-yard score. During the drive, we kept thinking, "Well, they won't run that play again." But they did, over and over again.

Doug Kay joined our staff in 1980 as our defensive coordinator. In 1982, he added "associate head coach" to his job titles. In my view, Doug was one of the greatest coaches we ever had at Hawaiʻi. He later became head coach for the Charlotte Rage and Carolina Cobras of the Arena Football League. In fact, he's still active in the league, serving as the defensive coordinator and associate head coach of the Tampa Bay Storm.

Doug was a master of putting defenses together, but even he was bewildered by BYU's effective ground game. "This time, it wasn't their quarterback or their defense, like in the past," he told *The Honolulu Advertiser* after the game. "This time, they just drew and trapped successfully inside against us. We understood we might see it. We just weren't capable of stopping it."

The Cougars won the game, 39-25.

Now, let's get to the 1984 game.

Talent-wise, our 1984 team was as good as it gets. We had Raphel Cherry back at quarterback after a record-setting junior season. Walter Murray, possessing both size (6-4) and speed (4:39 in the 40), was already considered perhaps the best receiver in the history of our program. And our defense was led by senior safety Rich Miano, along with a talented redshirt freshman named Al Noga.

Add to the mix players like receiver Mike Akiu, running back Nuʻu Faʻaola, tight end Ron Hall, linebackers M.L. Johnson and Pete Noga, defensive back Kent

Kafentzis, offensive linemen Joe Onosai and Mark Nua, and defensive lineman Colin Scotts.

That's thirteen players on our 1984 roster that went on to play in the NFL.

Despite our talent, we stumbled out of the gate to open our season. We were upset by Cal State Fullerton in our opener, then lost to Colorado State in Fort Collins in our first conference game. So we were 0-2 heading into our battle with BYU.

I started getting calls from *kāhuna* and other spiritual people, all offering suggestions to help the team. I tried to be as appreciative as I could, but I felt that all we had to do was play a little better.

Here again, I want to point out how amazing our fans were. Despite our poor start, 50,000 fans showed up at Aloha Stadium to see us play the No. 4-ranked Cougars.

Steve Young was no longer with BYU. He had moved on to the professional ranks, playing for the Los Angeles Express of the fledgling United States Football League. But, once again, Lavell Edwards had another ace up his sleeve in junior quarterback Robbie Bosco.

BYU led 12-0 in the second quarter before our special teams unit finally got us on the scoreboard. David Aguilar (now Dyas) blocked a Cougar punt and recovered the ball in the end zone for six points. Richard Spelman's extra point made it 12-7. Just a few minutes later, with 1:44 left in the first half, Richard booted a 33-yard field goal to draw us closer.

Both teams were held scoreless in the third quarter, setting up the dramatic final period. Ralph led our offense on an 84-yard, 21-play drive, culminating with another Richard Spelman field goal. That drive included big runs by Nu'u Fa'aola and Marco Johnson, and a key 9-yard reception by Walter Murray. Our offensive line—Joe Onosai, Brian Derby, Quentin Flores, Darryl Ursery, Raschad Galimba and Theo Adams—did a great job of protecting Ralph and creating holes for our running backs.

At one point during the drive, we had a first down just inside BYU's 2-yard line. We tried a couple of quarterback sneaks, but were stopped. On third and goal, BYU's Kyle Morrell leaped over our line, flipped over and corralled Ralph by the jersey. Morrell timed his leap perfectly. To this day, BYU fans regard that moment as the greatest defensive play in their program's history. (If you want to see that play, it's on YouTube.)

Still, with the field goal, we were now up, 13-12.

BYU battled back, as champions do. They went on an 80-yard, 6-play drive of their own, except they finished with a touchdown. Wide receiver Glen Kozlowski had tortured us all night, snaring 9 passes for 156 yards. His 25-yard touchdown grab from Bosco put the Cougars back on top, 18-13, with just 5:24 left in the game.

BYU got the ball back and was looking to run out the clock, but our defense stiffened and forced the Cougars to punt the ball deep in their own territory. Then Al Noga created a little bit of Hālawa magic.

In a play that brought back fond memories of his older brother Niko, Al broke through the line of scrimmage and rushed punter Lee Johnson. When Al blocked the kick, the entire stadium erupted. Suddenly, we had the ball on BYU's 10-yard line with 1:01 left to play!

Freshman running back Junior Lopati advanced the ball 2 yards on first down. On second down, with no one open, Ralph wisely threw the ball away. On third down, Ralph tried to get the ball to tight end Shephard Killen, but the pass was overthrown.

Now it was fourth down, and the clock was ticking. Ralph dropped back, stepped forward and fired a pass to Walter Murray in the end zone. In that split second, it seemed everyone in the entire state of Hawai'i breathed a collective gasp.

Walter stretched out and reached for the ball. He got a hand on it.

The ball bounced off his hands and fell harmlessly to the turf.

Final score: BYU 18, Hawai'i 13.

Brian Derby: *That loss stung. In my mind, I thought we were the better team.*

Walter Murray: *It was just one of those things. If you make the catch, you're a hero. But if you miss the catch, it becomes something you think about forever. I definitely still think about that play. I don't know if most athletes are like this, but I generally think more about the failures than the times where everything went right. I think, "If I had just done this" or "If I had just done that." Even when I was in the NFL, I wished that I'd learned how to dive for the ball. I dropped a similar pass when I was with the [Indianapolis] Colts.*

The hurt we felt after the game—I still have a hard time putting it into words. I even told the media to wait a while before entering the locker room. "Don't go in there," I said. "Let them recover."

We had put everything on the line in this game, and to come out on the losing end was the worst feeling in the world. "There were bodies flying all over the [field]," I told *Honolulu Advertiser* writer Dave Koga before joining my team. "I saw guys spill their guts all over the field. Their hearts and souls. We believed we could win, but we didn't. These guys' hearts are broken right now, but they'll be back tomorrow."

After seeing the tears and sobs that filled our locker room, however, I wasn't so sure about that last part.

"Guys, I just need to take a minute," I said. Then I left the locker room to gather myself. I was crying, too.

We were now 0-3 for the season. We knew we had a good team, but we couldn't prove it. Beating BYU would have been the perfect remedy to get us back on track.

When you're a head coach, when you see your team totally down and looking inconsolable, it's your job to lift them up. You have to say something that makes sense to them, something that will help them recover because, in our case, we still had eight games left to play. The season was not over.

I walked back into the locker room and addressed the team.

"I want everybody to look around this locker room," I said. "Look at everybody around you."

The guys looked around for a bit, then dropped their heads again.

"No," I said, my voice rising. "I want you to *really* look at each other. Get your heads up. We're going to come back from this thing. Look at each other, and you'll see what I see. The only positive thing about this, the one thing that we can feel good about, is that we're all feeling so bad about this game. And if we truly feel this way, then we can work together to find a way to make things better. We can make it so that, at the end of the season, we won't even remember this freaking game.

"When you leave this locker room, everybody outside is going to try to console you and tell you, 'That's okay.' It's not okay. We had a chance to win this game, but we didn't. Did we give a great effort? Yes. Was it good enough? No, it wasn't. We're all disappointed, but don't be discouraged. If we're discouraged, we won't be able to come back from this."

I didn't sleep that night. In fact, I didn't sleep for the next couple of days.

The day after the loss, we gathered as a team to look over the game film. It was about five o'clock in the afternoon. Something drastic needed to be done, and I knew what I wanted to do. I would utilize a tactic that would eventually be known as the Marathon Encounter.

"Rather than look at this tape, I want to talk to every one of you guys individually," I announced. "I don't care if this takes all night. Whether you played every down or didn't play at all, I need to talk to you. I want to look you right in the eye. I want to tell you what I think, and I want you to tell me what you think. I want you to tell me how you feel."

And so that's what we did. I stayed up all night and talked to every one of our players. Some of the guys were concerned because we were 0-3, and we were a much better team than that. Was our season lost? How do we come back from this?

The biggest thing that I wanted each player to know was that I had been there before. I had been on teams that had rough starts. And I had seen teams turn their season completely around.

"What I want you to understand is that we need more from you," I said. "What you've been giving is not good enough. We're 0-3. We need more from every single person. We need more from every player and every coach. We're going to come back from this. I know we can do this."

That week, I had our coaches put up arrows, pointing upward, all over the place. We placed them in the bathrooms, inside the lockers—everywhere the players went, they saw arrows pointing upward. The message was clear: onward and upward.

By midweek, I had never been so tired in my life. At the same time, however, I had never been so excited in my life! I knew we had it within ourselves to recover from this.

And we did. We won the next seven games. We beat UNLV, which had Randall Cunningham at quarterback. We beat Fresno State, which also had a great team. We beat UTEP down in El Paso. We beat Utah.

Larry Goeas: *After that BYU game, we could have folded and quit. But we were just so pissed off. Everybody got together and said, "There's no bleeping way this season is over. We fought back and took things one game at a time. We were in some close games, games where we easily could have lost, but somebody always made something happen—a blocked punt, a big first down or a goal line stand. Coach kept saying, "Some way, somehow, we're going to win this game."*

As for BYU, you could say that they finished their season strong as well. They completed their regular season a perfect 12-0, then defeated Michigan in the Holiday Bowl to win the national title. I was happy for my friend, Lavell Edwards, as well as the rest of the team. They represented our conference like the champions they were. There were several Hawaiʻi-born players on that Cougars roster, including Kurt Gouveia, Lakei Heimuli, Ladd Akeo, Robert Anae and Thor Salanoa. Of course, another individual with Hawaiʻi connections was future UH head coach Norm Chow, who at the time called the offensive plays for BYU.

And yes, Lavell Edwards was my friend. I forget what year it was, but WAC commissioner Joe Kearney sent Lavell and me to New York City one summer to meet with all the television executives. We got to spend three or four days together, and we really got to know each other. Our friendship grew over time, as we spent time together during our WAC meetings.

Eventually, Coach Edwards became one of my dearest friends. Our friendship transcended football and all the games that we played. As successful as he was, Lavell never had the air of somebody who thought he was better than everybody else. He was a tremendous competitor and a gracious winner. He was just a good human being. (When Bob Wagner became UH head coach, he said he was determined not to like Coach Edwards. I don't think he succeeded!)

One of the passions that we shared was golf. In fact, I'll let you in a little secret: Lavell and I frequently golfed together—sometimes the day before our game!

We played at Waiʻalae Country Club. We'd play nine holes early in the day, usually seven o'clock, so that we'd be done by 8:30 or so. We played in Provo a couple of times, too, but usually the temperatures were too cold.

Lavell said, "We can't ever tell people about this." He thought that people would think it was strange that we'd be socializing like this. And we sure as heck couldn't tell people we were out golfing the day before our football game!

Once, we were playing nine holes at Wai'alae, and the ninth hole was right in front of Alec Waterhouse's home. Alec was one of the founding fathers of Koa Anuenue, the fundraising arm of UH athletics. He was also the CEO of one of Hawai'i's largest companies and one of the most philanthropic people you could ever meet.

Alec and I were good friends. In fact, Alec owned a beautiful home in Kula on the island of Maui, and he would make it available for our entire coaching staff during the summers. We'd take up to twenty people there and enjoy everything that the island had to offer. My daughter, Angie, gained her deep appreciation for farming and nature from the property's caretaker, Aiko. Those two would walk and talk for hours!

Anyway, Lavell and I made our tee shots and starting walking down the fairway. As we were chatting, here comes Alec walking toward us from his backyard gate. He was wearing an old pair of shirts and a T-shirt. Lavell sees Alec and asks me, "Who's this guy?"

I decided to have some fun. "Oh, it's my caddy," I said. I said it loud enough that Alec could hear it. Sure enough, Alec was happy to play along.

"Hey, Dick. How are you guys doing?" he said, waving.

I introduced Lavell to my "caddy," and the three of us had a nice conversation. After a while, Alec left us to return to his house. Only then did I tell Lavell who he really was.

"That man owns more property in the state of Hawai'i than anybody I know," I said with a smile. We both got a good laugh out of that.

Here's the kicker: After he retired from coaching, Lavell wrote a book. The same guy who said we could never tell anyone about our golf outings penned an entire chapter about the two of us playing golf together!

Coach Edwards passed away in December 2016, and it kills me that he's gone. I miss him dearly.

After the 1984 game, I was 0-6 against BYU. I was always considered a positive thinker, but even I began wondering if we could ever beat our biggest rival.

In 1985, we lost to the Cougars, 26-6, to cap a disappointing 4-6-1 season. In that game, their halfback, Vai Sikahema, shredded our defense. The future NFL star had 86 yards rushing in only 11 carries, and 198 receiving yards on 12 receptions. He scored two touchdowns, including an 80-yard hookup with Robbie Bosco.

Walter Murray: *I still hate Vai Sikahema!*

The next year, we fell again to BYU. It was our homecoming game, and we lost

10-3. Ultimately, it was that game that helped us decide that a change was needed. We had to find a way to be more unpredictable offensively when we played a team like BYU, which was too good at defending conventional offenses. We needed to do something different conceptually to give us a better chance to win.

We needed an offense with more juice. We needed a different style of attack.

I'll explore this subject a lot more in Chapter Eight, but I think you already know where I'm going with this.

Looking back, our games against BYU, even though we lost them all during my UH tenure, were so valuable in the building of our program. We learned so much from these contests. And in the end, we gained their respect. They knew that it was only a matter of time before we'd come out on top.

I promise you, when Coach Wags' team beat BYU in 1989, every person that had any Rainbow Warrior blood in them was celebrating. Nobody on our previous teams was upset because they never got to achieve that elusive win. Everybody celebrated, and rightfully so. It was the moment we had all been waiting for!

Chapter Seven

FAN-TASTIC!

WHENEVER PEOPLE BRING UP THE so-called "Dick Tomey era" of University of Hawai'i football, they inevitably point to the great players who gave their all to the program. And there is no question that we had many outstanding student-athletes in my ten years at the university. Other fans might point to the upsets and near-upsets we had against the likes of USC and Michigan.

But when I relive that particular decade of Rainbow Warrior football, I tell everyone the same thing: The fans are the true heroes of this story.

The numbers don't lie. More than 3.4 million fans came to our home games during my UH tenure. In 1984, we set a school attendance record for the most games of 40,000 or more at home, with nine. The three largest average home attendance records in our program's history came during my final three seasons at UH: 1984 (45,765), 1986 (44,905) and 1985 (44,880). Five of our games were complete sellouts.

It didn't matter if we played big-name opponents or lesser-known teams. We drew more than 46,000 for our 1980 season opener against Abilene Christian, for example. In 1983, more than 46,000 fans showed up at Aloha Stadium to see us play Long Beach State, which doesn't even have a football program anymore.

Most impressive of all, the Hawai'i fans came out to support us even when we were struggling. We started our 1984 season 0-3, including the devastating 18-13 home loss to BYU. In Week Four, however, nearly 42,000 fans showed up for our home game against UNLV. The week after that, another 42,000 fans attended our game against Fresno State.

When we had stretches of exhilarating success, our fans were right there along for the ride. Every time we were down, those same fans were right there to pick us up.

Rick Blangiardi (UH player, 1965-66; linebackers coach, 1972-73; associate head coach/defensive coordinator, 1974-76): *I'll give you an idea of what attendance was like during the Dick Tomey years: [UH athletic director] Stan Sheriff and I were best friends, and we used to sit down for beers and talk for* hours. We would talk about Aloha Stadium. This was when the stadium was still portable and could go from baseball to football. We talked about configuring it permanently to football and filling in the spaces next to the end zones. We even had some architectural designs in place to figure out how many additional people we could put in. It was about 4,000 fans per puka. Now, that never happened, obviously. But back then, it seemed that 50,000 seats weren't enough.

Falaniko Noga: *All my four years at UH, the fans came out and believed in us. I remember that every time I walked into the stadium there was a group that called themselves "Noga's Togas"—something like that. They all wore togas and cheered like crazy for us. Just walking on the field before the game, they would chant my name. I guess they appreciated my hard work and believed in what I could do. I really enjoyed it.*

Gary Allen: *I love the Hawai'i fans. Even today, they come up to me and say, "Gary, you were my favorite player." Or they'll ask if they can take a picture with me. That kind of stuff. I love it. It's very humbling to me.*

Of course, I still root for the Rainbows. A lot of us former players, we attend a lot of the games. Rick Nakashima, who was a coach for the UH track team, used to hang out with us. When UH goes on the road to play UNLV, Rick comes out to Los Angeles, rents a bus at the airport, picks us up and takes us all to Las Vegas. We always have a great time!

David Toloumu: *We were celebrities in the Islands, and people really welcomed us. I got love everywhere I went. We would walk around Ala Moana Center, and kids would come up and ask for our autographs. It felt great.*

Jim Asmus: *Every time I come back to Hawai'i, it honestly feels like coming home again. I have friendships over there that I value as much as the friendships I have here [in California], if not more so. The people of Hawai'i took me in and gave me a neat experience. I remember after home games, we'd go to the tailgates and talk to the people. We'd also go to the schools to reach out to the kids. I have nothing but good things to say about the people of Hawai'i.*

Nu'u Fa'aola: *The fans? Oh, my goodness! I remember Jim Leahey asking me how it felt to hear forty or fifty thousand fans chanting my first name? Well, when they first started doing that, it sounded like they were booing me. On the field, I was thinking, "Why are they booing me? I'm doing the best that I can." But I loved playing for our fans. It felt like the team was carrying the entire state on our backs. The adrenaline just flowed. What a motivation for us!*

Brian Derby: *I remember our 1984 game against San Diego State. That was the game Junior Lopati blew out his knee after a late hit in the end zone after a 62-yard touchdown run. It was also the first time that the fans at Aloha Stadium got the Wave going. They had tried to do it all season, and they finally did it! I remember standing at our 40-yard line when the Wave started going around the stadium. I was, like, "No bleeping way! Yeah! Yeaahhhh!"*

Early on, it was clear that our team and the Hawai'i fans had formed a special connection—a "Rainbow Connection," if you will—and that bond only grew stronger as my time at UH went on.

Why did the fans embrace the Rainbow Warriors in record numbers? Well, for one thing, it was just a very exciting time for Hawai'i football. It was unprecedented. We had joined the Western Athletic Conference, which was a high-level league with schools such as BYU, Utah and San Diego State. Our schedule was upgraded to include nationally ranked opponents just about every year. Aloha Stadium was still a relatively new facility. All of those things combined to create an explosion of energy that Hawai'i fans fed off of.

Another part of it, I think, had to do with the makeup of our team. While we were able to bring in some quality players that other schools coveted, we also had walk-on players that local people could easily relate to. Hawai'i fans love to root for the scrappy underdog that fights and claws and scratches his way to the top. They love rags-to-riches stories.

One of our earliest walk-ons, and one of our greatest success stories, was Larry Goeas. Larry came to us out of Kaiser High School. His first season, in 1979, he was our Scout of the Year. The next year, he was named Warrior of the Year.

Larry Goeas: *I'd had a disappointing senior season at Kaiser. My dad and I talked, and the plan was to sit out a year and do weight training to build my strength. I was actually planning to go to the mainland and play at Linfield College. But then Dad said, "Why don't you just walk on at UH?" I found a phone book and got the number for the football program. Then I made a cold call to Coach Tomey. I said, "Hi, Coach. My name is Larry Goeas…"*

That first year, I was on the scout team so I didn't have the pressure of having to play in the games. That was the year we played USC and almost ruined their hopes for the national championship. I was on the sidelines watching Tom Tuinei just eat up their All-American tackle, Keith Van Horne.

Another walk-on was Sam Moku, a tremendous athlete who had played football, soccer and track at Damien. In fact, Sam is the subject of one of my favorite stories, which I enjoy sharing a lot. File this one under "Everyone Can Contribute in Different Ways."

Sam Moku (UH defensive back, 1983-86): *Yeah, it's a story that Dick always talks about. It was our 1984 game against San Diego State. The Aztecs had a wide receiver, Webster Slaughter, who was having a great year. Back then, San Diego State was as much of a rival for us as BYU was. They were hard to beat.*

It happened so fast. In the middle of the second quarter, San Diego State had a running play. The tackle was made, and everyone sprinted toward the pile because coaches taught us to swarm to the ball. Anyway, I'm running towards the pile and suddenly Webster Slaughter comes up and hits me on the side. I turned around and pushed him back, and we got into a little scuffle. It wasn't a huge fight, maybe just a couple of quick jabs here and there.

The referees came in to separate us. Yellow flags were everywhere. I didn't think much of it, but all of a sudden I got called to the sideline. That's when the referee announced, "Number 40, he's out!" I was ejected from the game.

Then the referee said, "Number 88, he's also out!" And the crowd just roared! They were happy that San Diego State's best player was out of the game!

I remember when Sam returned to the sidelines. I pulled him aside and said, "Great job!" I also told him that if we won the game, I'd give him the game ball. (And we did win, 16-10.) Slaughter went on to play twelve years in the NFL, earning All-Pro honors with the Cleveland Browns.

Of course, our walk-ons also contributed in more conventional ways. In 1982, we played a big game against Utah. This was the same contest that Raphel Cherry made the greatest play I ever saw a quarterback make that wasn't a pass or a run. (See Chapter Five.)

Our starting kicker, Lee Larsen, was out with an injury, and we held a contest before the game to decide who would kick our field goals. The winner was a walk-on named Richard Spelman, who had joined the team a couple of years earlier out of Radford High School.

We were locked in a 7-7 tie with the Utes late in the fourth quarter. We had the ball and were trying to get in position to kick a field goal to win the game. There was less than a minute to play, and it was fourth down. I yell, "Field goal!" and everybody on the kicking unit sprinted onto the field.

Except for Richard Spelman!

Richard was just standing on the sideline. I barked, "Spelman! Get your ass in there!"

Bless his heart, Richard runs up to me and asks, "Coach, is it still me?"

He thought that maybe I'd let someone else kick it. (In his defense, it had only been four hours since he'd won our kicking contest.)

Richard ran in, we snapped the ball, and the 37-yard kick was absolutely perfect. We won the game, 10-7. It was Richard's only field goal attempt that season. He later told me that he was glad he didn't have time to think about his kick. It was a very pressure-packed situation, and he delivered.

Brian Derby: *Here's another walk-on for you: Richard Higa. He and I were teammates at Pearl City High. Richard was one of the toughest guys around. He never missed a practice at UH. He took some cracks! That's why we called him "Timex." He took a licking and kept on ticking!*

Dino Babers: *Man, Richard was everybody's favorite. The fans at the stadium used to chant his name all the time. "Higa! Higa! Higa!"*

Perhaps the greatest success story in the history of our walk-on program belongs to Rich Miano. In retrospect, it's almost inconceivable that a two-time All-WAC performer and ten-year NFL veteran never even got a look from college football recruiters.

Rich Miano (UH defensive back, 1982-84): *It was 1978, and I had just moved to Hawai'i from the mainland. I wasn't playing football at the time because I was feeling miserable here, and I was being kind of rebellious. On a whim, I accepted an invitation to watch the Hawai'i-USC game. I saw how Hawai'i battled, and I saw the fan support—there were 50,000 people at Aloha Stadium. I told myself, "Man, if I ever get good enough to play college football, why would I go anywhere else?"*

I wasn't good enough at the time. Nobody wanted me. I was set to go to Willamette or Linfield or maybe some junior college on the west coast. But then my brother, Robert, died in a tragic accident at Spitting Caves in Hawai'i Kai. He and I were inseparable, and he was my best friend. I felt like I needed to stay home for my family.

At UH, I had mentors like Mark Kafentzis and Blane Gaison. I watched how hard they worked. Being a walk-on, I had to make sure I worked harder than everybody else. I had some legendary workouts, and to be honest, I probably over-trained. Our strength coach was Terry Albritton, who had been the world record holder in the shot put. He was the first man to throw a shotput seventy feet. Terry got us to do plyometrics before it became popular. He got us to do explosive-type training. I truly believe that this skinny, slow, white defensive back would never have made it to the NFL without being able to take [Terry's] knowledge and use it to end up with a 36-inch vertical jump and a 4.5 40-yard dash, plus being able to bench 220 pounds twenty or more times. Also, my technique wouldn't have been good as it was if it weren't for Bob Wagner and Duane Akina.

Bob Wagner: *In the beginning, Rich was really, really raw. When I saw him backpedal for the first time, he looked so bad that I had to turn my back to hide my smile. He was trying so hard, but he just didn't look very good. But Rich just got better every year.*

Rich Miano: *I think the blue-collar people of Hawai'i just became enamored with that whole generation of great walk-on players. The fans appreciated the guys who maybe weren't as big or fast or strong. We just got out there and battled. As the first walk-on to make the NFL, I feel like the Pied Piper. So many great walk-ons came afterward: the Mike Treslers, David Maevas, John Veneris and Eddie Klaneskis. Later, when June Jones took over the program, he made me the team's walk-on coordinator. We had guys like Ashley Lelie, James Fenderson, Travis Laboy—even Colt Brennan started here as a walk-on.*

And it all started with Coach Tomey.

Sam Moku: *When I graduated from Damien, I didn't even know what a walk-on was. The guy who really helped me get on the team was [UH linebacker] Alvis Satele. I used to watch all the Satele boys play at Castle High because I lived right next to the school's football field. Alvis was the one who got me to meet Rich Ellerson. Coach Ellerson just told me to sign up.*

All the walk-ons, we had heart. We went 110 percent all the time. We were determined to help the program, no matter what. Coach Tomey and all of the other coaches really cultivated that. They could tell there was a difference between the walk-ons having to fight for their jobs versus the players who were given scholarships. They could tell who was putting out and who wasn't. As walk-ons, we just had to persevere and tough it out.

One of the greatest examples of the deep connection between our team and the people of Hawai'i is the Senior Walk. It began as a spontaneous outpouring of aloha from the fans to our seniors, and over the years it evolved into a heartfelt tradition that is truly unique to Hawai'i. Unfortunately, like so many other things, the Senior Walk became commercialized in later years and lost much of its spontaneity and allure.

The player who started it all was Nelson Maeda, a steady and dependable defensive back who came to our program from Kailua High School. His last game for us was our big upset over Arizona State in 1979.

Blane Gaison: *We had just finished the game, and I was sitting by my locker, putting my stuff away. At this point, most of the guys had already showered. Nelson Maeda came running into the locker room. I said, "You haven't taken a shower yet? Where'd you go?" And Nelson said, "I just had to take one last run around the field."*

The next year was my senior season, and after the last game we headed to the locker room. Now, usually after the games I would go outside to thank the security guards, the ushers and other people that worked on the field. I started to walk back out to the field and Eddie Riewerts asked, "Where are you going?" I said, "Ed, why don't you come with me? Let's go take one more walk."

So we walked back to the field and started thanking the stadium workers. Jim Leahey and Rick Blangiardi were doing their postgame radio show, and they announced, "There's Blane Gaison and Eddie Riewerts, the two captains. They're back on the field." The next thing you know, fans started coming back into the stadium. It was great! Afterward, Jim asked me, "What was that all about?" And I said, "We just wanted to thank the people who supported us over the years. We wanted to take one final walk around the stadium. It's our last hurrah."

Little did I know that I was going to be back at Aloha Stadium just a few weeks later, playing in the Hula Bowl. But that was my last hurrah as a Rainbow Warrior. That's how [the Senior Walk] started.

Another reason for our tremendous fan support was Aloha Stadium itself. The stadium first opened its gates to the public on September 12, 1975. The 50,000-seat facility was the first of its kind to feature four movable sections. It could alternate between football and baseball configurations, and for several years we shared the venue with the Hawai'i Islanders baseball team.

Aloha Stadium was still practically brand new when I arrived in Hawai'i in 1977. June Jones recently told me that he thinks a lot of our fan support was due to the newness of the facility. Some high school games at the time drew between 25,000 and 30,000 people. Clearly, football fans enjoyed coming out to the stadium.

I understand that the late John A. Burns, who served as Hawai'i's governor from 1962 to 1974, was a big advocate for its construction. In fact, Governor Burns was a great supporter of UH athletics in general, donating $8,000 of his own money to help kickstart 'Ahahui Koa Ānuenue, the official fundraising arm of the UH athletic department.

Rich Ellerson: *I think Governor Burns saw the possibilities of what football could mean to the people of Hawai'i and our culture. Aloha Stadium and Division I football were part of the Governor's vision. For a long time, football games at the stadium were a real gathering. The games were a part of it, but there was something else going on, too. There was a celebration of community that we all felt.*

There was that moment in time when it all came together: the stadium, Governor Burns' vision, the transition to Division I and the uniqueness of our culture. And then there was Coach Tomey, who resonated with the best parts of our local culture.

As the people of Hawaiʻi reached out to us, we in turn reached out to them. We made every effort to get involved in the community. We visited schools and hospitals, and we tried to be an inspiration to future generations of Rainbow Warrior supporters.

Dino Babers: *I remember the Carole Kai Bed Race [benefiting the Variety School of Hawaiʻi for special-needs children]! We watched it the first year, and I think a military team won. We decided that we were going to enter the event the next year and not let them win anymore. It got to be a really good rivalry.*

One year, Don Ho's daughter was the young lady in our bed, and we were running for our sponsor, the Polynesian Palace. That was just a heck of a race! I was on the last leg. At first, we were just a bit behind the military guys. But coming down the final stretch we were running neck and neck. It was me, Jeff Breland, Tim Lyons and one other player—maybe Nate Fletcher. Anyway, the military team had moved a bit ahead of us when all of a sudden our team had this massive surge and we beat the military guys to the finish line. We were so excited!

Then I turned around and saw Tim Lyons running toward us. We were like, "Tim, what happened?" And he said, "I was holding you guys back, so I just let go."

Yeah, Timmy wasn't the fastest guy in the world.

Our football program also benefited from increased media exposure, which came in several different forms. We had *The Dick Tomey Show*, a one-hour TV program that aired on KHON throughout my term as UH coach. A lot of people don't know this, but that show was live every Sunday. We were probably the only coach's show in America that was live, not taped.

Joe Moore co-hosted the show for a year or two, and then I co-hosted the program with Les Keiter. One year, for reasons I can't remember, I hosted the show by myself.

For UH fans, the TV show was an opportunity to relive highlights from the previous night's game. Viewers tuned in to see the fantastic open-field runs by Gary Allen, the bone-crunching sacks by Niko Noga and the punt return exploits of Dana McLemore—all with commentary and insights by yours truly. But more than that, the program also included these wonderful human interest features of our players. These vignettes showed a personal side of our players that the public rarely got to see.

Al Hoffman (producer and director, *The Dick Tomey Show*, 1977-86): *I was the station's program director at the time. I was a sports fan, so I pretty much did it for fun. To capture the game highlights, we shot everything on film. We would shoot slow-motion at the field level, and we also had a camera shooting from above. Then we'd go running back after the game and edit the film for most of the night.*

The whole crew loved doing the show. Dick was a class act, and he treated every-

body well. When we ran the highlights, he would talk over the action, and it never ceased to amaze me how much insight he would add. He would talk about things that weren't obvious to the average fan. He'd say things like, "The right side of our line had a dominant game" or "Our defensive tackles were the key to our defense." It really made the show interesting.

I know Dick really liked the in-depth profiles. I would go down to the practices during the week and talk with him and the other coaches, and they'd offer suggestions on players to feature. There were some really surprising stories. Some of the players were married. Some had rough backgrounds. Some were dealing with being a long way from home. The profiles were fun to do, and they kind of humanized the players for the fans.

The ratings were very good. We had huge numbers. Advertising sales-wise, we always sold out. Of course, in those days we didn't have cable TV like we do now. And it certainly helped that the show was on from four to five o'clock, right before one of the great institutions at KHON, Let's Go Fishing.

The sad thing is, the shows weren't archived or stored properly. I've looked over the years, but as far as I know everything is gone. I don't think the shows were ever transferred to tape. We just didn't think about it at that time.

Even my son, Rich, got some television exposure. During our games, Rich had the important task of holding the cord for my headset so it wouldn't get snarled or tangled. Once, he was interviewed on TV by a reporter who asked him what it was like carrying the cord around for Dad.

His reply: "It's just like walking the dog."

Yes, Rich really said that!

Then the TV segment showed a tape of me walking on the sideline, with Rich holding the cord behind me. Suddenly, the ball went the other way and Rich stopped and tugged the cord in the other direction, turning me completely around!

I would be remiss if I neglected to mention the great job that the KHNL/KFVE crew did in broadcasting our games on TV. As play-by-play announcers go, few were better than Jim Leahey. He's a pro's pro, and he was a tremendous asset to our program.

I also enjoyed the analyst work of Rick Blangiardi. He had played and coached at UH, and his insights added a lot to the broadcasts.

Rick Blangiardi: *Jim and I made no bones about being homers. In those days, we were the producers of record. So when we played Iowa, for example, Iowa had to use our broadcast. We were on the Hawkeye Network. We probably pissed off all those Iowa fans, but we made no pretense about what we did.*

Dick was notorious for being conservative on offense. There was one game where he seemed preoccupied with running Nuʻu Faʻaola up the middle. It was a fullback dive play, and it wasn't going anywhere. It was as though Nuʻu was running into a wall.

Now, I had always made a pact with myself that I would never second-guess the coaches on the air. I had too much respect for the profession. As a former coach, I knew that the margin between winning and losing was very thin.

But that night, after about twelve attempts of Nuʻu running up the middle, I said, "I don't know why Coach Tomey is insisting on running that play. It's going absolutely nowhere." Then, in the very next series, Nuʻu broke it up the middle and ran something like 80 yards for a touchdown!

I remember saying, "Well, gag me with a towel!" That run broke the game open, and Hawaiʻi went on to win the game. The coaches knew what they were doing, and their persistence paid off.

Here's one bit of trivia for you: UH football was featured on the very day that Prime Ticket Network [now Fox Sports West] made its debut. We formed a partnership with Jerry Buss, who owned the Los Angeles Lakers, and a guy named Bill Daniels. Prime Ticket was the first of the regional sports networks, and we broadcast the Hawaiʻi-Pacific football game on that first day.

Finally, there was my TV commercial for Grand Pacific Insurance, the life insurance company founded and headed by the late businessman and politician Wadsworth Yee. It's the only commercial spot I ever did, and it was my introduction into how much detail goes into an endeavor like that. We flew to Los Angeles to tape it, and, believe it or not, it took three days to do that one thirty-second spot!

That commercial ran for a long time, and people still mention it to me today. I guess you could say it was my acting debut. Although I enjoyed the experience, I knew I wasn't about to challenge Robert De Niro for any Academy Awards.

Likening my acting ability to that of a famous Hollywood legend?

It's like comparing apples and oranges.

Chapter Eight

WHAT WE LEARNED

In football, as in life, one thing is certainly true: You never stop learning. From the moment I first diagrammed a defensive scheme to the day I hung up my whistle and clipboard, I never stopped evolving as a football coach. Even today, I'm learning new things about this game that I love and have so much passion for.

My ten seasons as head coach of the University of Hawai'i Rainbow Warriors was a continuous learning process, both for the coaching staff and for the players. The lessons we learned together helped us to overcome obstacles, manage adversities and win games. Many of these lessons helped us to grow both on and off the football field.

For example, we learned how to be a better road team. In my first couple of seasons in Hawai'i, we weren't very successful playing away from the confines of Aloha Stadium. In fact, it wasn't until our sixth road game that we were able to pull out a victory (a convincing 27-12 win over UTEP in El Paso).

I've always believed that you're not at a disadvantage when you go on the road unless you think you are. But it was clear to me after our first few road games that we didn't really understand how to travel as effectively as we needed to. Road trips for the Rainbow Warriors weren't like USC going across town to visit UCLA, or BYU bussing it from Provo to Salt Lake City to play Utah. Every trip we took required, at minimum, a five-hour flight across the Pacific Ocean.

One year, we made it a point to visit the Olympic Training Center in Colorado Springs. The state-of-the-art facility is still the flagship training center for the United States Olympic Committee and several of its teams.

We solicited the advice of the experts, and they gave us some good ideas. For one thing, we changed our eating habits while we were on the road. We had been eating too much. It was better that our players eat less and drink more fluids. That didn't make me very popular with the guys—football players love their food!—but our approach did bring positive results. (And we fed them a lot after the game!) After our 0-5 road start, the Rainbow Warriors went 13-9-1 away from home for the rest of my UH tenure.

We were also advised to stay on Hawai'i time. We were assured that it was fine for

Defensive back Kent Kafentzis was one of eight members of the same Washington state family to don a Rainbow Warriors uniform.

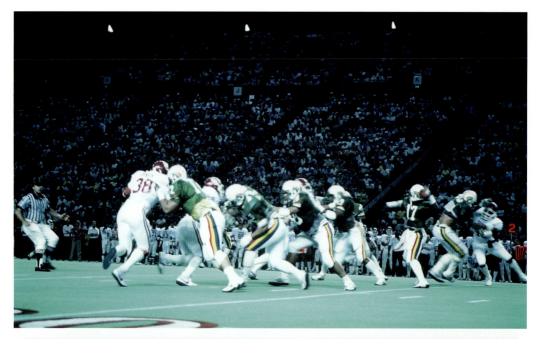

Both the UH offense (top) and defense had outstanding games in the Rainbow Warriors' close loss to Oklahoma in 1983.

Top: Running back Richard Higa, a Pearl City High School alum, was a fan favorite at Aloha Stadium. **Above:** The 1984 Rainbow Warriors lost its first three gut-wrenching games, then won seven in a row. The '84 team set the Rainbow Warriors' all-time per-game average attendance record of 45,765, which still holds today.

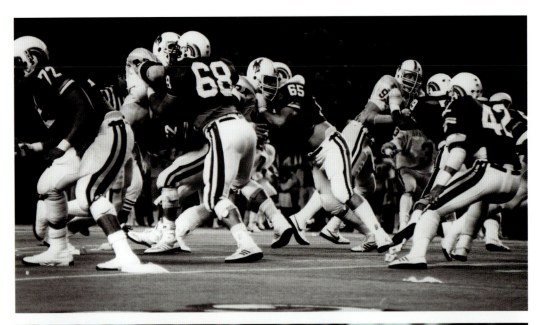

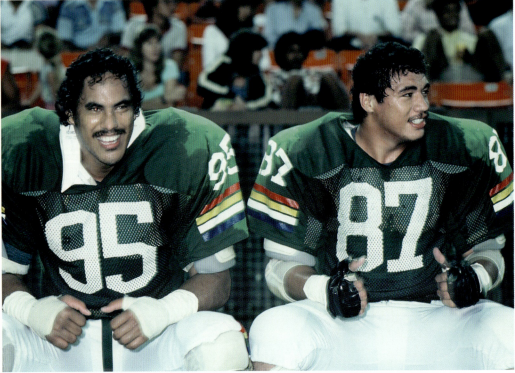

Top: Darryl Ursery, Brian Derby, Quentin Flores, Louis Santiago and others provide great pass protection against Wyoming. **Above:** Defensive linemen Emlen Kahoano and Kesi Afalava enjoy a tough game.

Top: In 1983 Raphel Cherry set twenty-two UH records in passing and total offense. **Above:** Rich Miano, Raphel, Walter Murray, Richard Spelman and Shepherd Killen after the Senior Walk in 1984.

Top: UH first-team All-American Al Noga sacks Michigan quarterback Jim Harbaugh in the 1986 season finale. **Above:** With the game tied at 10-10, Danny Crowell earns tough yardage in the fourth quarter against the eventual Rose Bowl champions.

Top: Gregg Tipton throws a pass in the Rainbow Warriors' 1986 upset of Wisconsin.
Above: George Fletcher hits a crack in this great comeback victory against the Badgers.

Top: Michigan head coach Bo Schembechler and Dick Tomey, 1986. **Above:** A packed Aloha Stadium, here in 1986, was a hallmark of the Tomey era in Rainbow Warrior football.

us to work really hard and then go to bed late. So that's what we did. In El Paso one year, we practiced at the Sun Bowl at midnight because it was still eight o'clock our time. The people who drove past the stadium probably thought we were crazy, but it worked. The players would go to bed tired, and the next day—game day—they got to sleep in a bit. When they woke up, they were rested and ready to take on the Miners.

Then, after the game, we left El Paso as soon as we could. That became our goal when we were on the road: Get in, get out.

We didn't mind playing on the road. We saw these games as unique challenges as well as terrific opportunities to see different places and encounter other cultures. Also, it was extremely satisfying to win a game in hostile territory.

Brian Derby: *During my senior season, we played at Wyoming in the snow. I don't know how it is now, but back then in Laramie the fans sat so close to the sidelines that they could almost touch you. As we ran out to the field, the fans were yelling at us and hurling insults our way. "Hey, Pineapple!" Of course, none of that bothered me. I just laughed.*

The Wyoming fans were relentless. They kept laughing and chirping at us the whole time. We won the game, and I thought we had the last laugh. But later, in the locker room, I took off my jersey and there was chewing tobacco juice all over my back. It was hilarious! Here I was, thinking that I got those guys, but they got me all freaking game by spitting on my back!

Larry Goeas: *The road trips were fun. I tell these stories to my kids all the time. We flew commercial, and usually Dick would have us in the last section of the plane. Guys like Steve Lehor and Kingman McCleod would mimic the flight attendants when they did their pre-flight routines. They would point to the exit windows, and then all fifty-four of us would point to the windows. After a while, even the flight attendants were cracking up!*

Of course, Coach always made sure that you were giving your best. One time, we lost on the road to Wyoming. On the flight to L.A. after the game, he noticed that some of the guys were horsing around. That bothered him. When we reached the hotel, he called a meeting. He said, "I know we only lost a game, but it has to mean more to you than horse-playing or joking around. Losing's got to hurt a little. It bothers me that it doesn't hurt you guys enough." And I knew what he meant.

On the field or behind the scenes, every college football team goes through peaks and valleys. In the BYU chapter, I mentioned our 1984 squad, which started the season 0-3, including an emotional loss to the Cougars, before winning seven straight games. Our 1981 team carried an eleven-game winning streak, then lost back-to-back contests.

Learning to deal with adversity and being able to move forward are essential if you want to succeed in life. Those are lessons I tried to impart to our players.

I often shared with the team my experience with one of my college psychology professors. One day, at the start of class, he showed us a painting of the Rocky Mountains. He pointed to it and said, "See this? That's your life. That's my life. That's the life of your business, your team, your organization and your family. That's the level of importance I'm attaching to this painting."

He looked around the classroom, and all he could see was perplexed faces.

"Hey, you guys go out and do what you do, and I'll see you again on Wednesday," he said. Then he smiled and added, "Of course, if you need to sit here for a while to look at the painting and figure out what in the world I mean, you're welcome to stay."

We were dumbfounded. First of all, the professor was letting us leave just five minutes after class had begun. But most of us didn't leave. We just sat there, trying to figure out the significance of the painting.

When we returned to class on Wednesday, everyone was still buzzing about the subject. It was only then that our professor gave us the explanation.

"See this?" he said, pointing to the very bottom of the evergreen valleys. "Notice, the vegetation is in the valley."

Okay.

"It means that the times of your greatest struggles, your deepest valleys, are the times when you grow the most. That's true of your life. It's true of my life. It's true for everybody and for everything. Think about it. If you look back on your life, it's those valleys you walked through that helped you grow the most as a person."

That lesson made a big impact on me. I can speak from experience that all the low points in my life have provided me opportunities for serious introspection. They've helped me to accept responsibility for my actions and figure out ways that I can do better. I've experienced so many ups and downs in my life. I've been hired and fired, and promoted and demoted. Through it all, the professor's wise instruction has helped me keep things in perspective, and I always tried to pass it on to the young men I've been blessed to coach and mentor.

I used to give my players a manual of my favorite sayings. They rarely read it at the time, I'm sure, but later on I've had players call me and say, "Coach, remember that book you gave us, and we'd put it away in our backpacks? I was in a tough spot, and I started reading those sayings. You know what? Those things you say are really meaningful."

One of my former players at Arizona once called me from Iraq. He was the head of a unit of Marines, and he shared with me a particularly harrowing experience. "We were all going to die," he said, "and I started thinking about all those things that were in that manual you gave us. Right after that, I started pulling all my guys together. All this stuff you used to say to us started to come out of me, and somehow we got out of there. I figured I should call you and thank you. Back when I was playing, I never paid much attention to those sayings."

That was understandable to me. When you're young, you don't yet have a lot of life experiences, so what a coach says to his players might not have a lot of meaning for them at that time. You just hope that the lessons you give them will help them later on in life, whether it involves football or not.

Blane Gaison: *If you ever played football, you know that there's nothing easy about the game. It's physical, it's hard, it's tough. But Coach Tomey reminded us that's how life is going to be. Life is going to be just like that. You're going to have good times and bad times, and no matter what happens you got to continue to push forward.*

There is no such thing as "quit." I learned that at the University of Hawai'i. I learned that as a Rainbow Warrior. Sometimes, your very best is not going to be good enough. But you know what? There's always another day. That's something that Coach Tomey and his staff always preached to us. I think that's why our program became so good at the time. We always tried to move forward and find ways to get better.

Jesse Sapolu: *One thing that Coach Tomey always emphasized to us was "The Team, The Team, The Team." We were taught to be selfless, not selfish. One day during my sophomore year, three guys had missed curfew. The next day, Coach Tomey brought three chairs to the field and placed them on the 10-yard line. He made those three guys sit on those chairs.*

Then, he had the rest of us gather in the end zone, and we had to do up-down drills for half an hour while those guys watched us. The guys who missed curfew didn't get punished, but the team got punished. Imagine that! There were guys dropping out and throwing up on the side. There was a message behind that: You let your brothers down by being selfish individuals. Those guys never broke curfew again.

Dino Babers: *One of the things that Coach Tomey used to say—and I can't get out of my head—was, "Pay attention to detail. It's the little things that make a difference." He repeated that to us so many times. He also said, "If you want to know what kind of coach you are, turn on the tape." And finally there's, "I want everybody to stand up, take your ego, fold it up, stick it in your back pocket and sit on it so we can get to work!"*

Joe Onosai: *Coach Tomey taught me about the importance of being punctual.*

My freshman year, when we were preparing for our first game, I was late for a team meeting. I walked into the room and Coach was already addressing the team. His steel blue eyes looked straight through me. I was in deep kimchee, man! Coach dug into me real good. The senior players like Niko Noga, Alvis Satele, Kesi Afalava and Embo Kahoano were giving me the stink eye. It was, like, "Come on, freshman. Get it together!" I'll never forget that. To this day, I don't like to be late.

Mark Kafentzis: *Coach always said, "If you want to play in the NFL, you better learn to play special teams. You can't be a prima donna and think you can just play your position." Because of that, I learned to love playing on special teams, and it helped me get to the NFL.*

Nu'u Fa'aola: *There's a favorite saying that Coach Tomey has that I first heard as a freshman. He said, "It's not the will to win. It's the will to prepare to win that separates those who wish and dream from those who make it happen." I still apply it to my life today, and I will use it until the day I die. I apply it to my relationships, I apply it to my marriage and I apply it to my work. Coach taught me about the value of hard work, and he knew that I would give every drop of sweat on my body for the team, program and state.*

I've always felt that you can have all the physical attributes in the world, but that won't guarantee you success in football. It also takes a firm belief that you can win. Sometimes, it's not even enough to believe you can win. You have to see it happening.

I first met Tony Robbins in 1984 when assistant coach Larry MacDuff and I attended his seminar at the Honolulu Club. At the time, Tony was just starting his journey as a successful motivational speaker, life coach, author, entrepreneur and philanthropist.

Before the session began, Tony led us to a bed of hot coals. He made us put our hands over them to feel how hot they were. Then he said, "In a few hours, we're going to come back out here and walk across these coals. And we're going to do it without fear."

A lot of Tony's talk focused on visualization, which is a significant thing for coaches and athletes. Afterward, we returned to the coals. Tony instructed us to keep our heads up and never look down. We were also told to say out loud, "Cool moss" repeatedly. More importantly, we were to visualize what we were saying.

Cool moss. Cool moss. Cool moss.

I did exactly as Tony instructed us, and I walked across the coals without burning my feet.

When we were done, Tony told us, "This is a metaphor for you. Use this to help yourself in different moments of your life. Now, you can stand in front of a crowd and make a speech. You can pursue your dream job. You can conquer cancer. You can be stronger than you think you are when you have to be."

Holy cow.

The fire walk, Tony explained, was a metaphor for getting fear out of your life. It was about visualizing yourself accomplishing your goals. "Don't look down," he repeated. "When you're looking up, you're in a certain state of mind. When you look down, you take yourself out of that state. (Over the ensuing years, I did the fire walk three more times. The last time I did it, I couldn't help but peek down during my last step. I burned the heck out of my right foot!")

Later, I asked Tony if he would consider putting our team through the fire walk and he agreed.

There were a few players who didn't feel comfortable doing it, and that was fine. We weren't about to force anyone to walk over the coals. But most of the guys did it, and they felt it was a great experience.

Marco Johnson (UH running back/wide receiver, 1983-87): *For three or four hours, Tony Robbins had us visualize ourselves doing incredible things: flying, running through brick walls, walking barefoot on hot coals, that sort of thing. Then he took us outside. About ten minutes later, I'm walking across a twenty-foot bed of hot coals! From that point forward, it's been my mantra that I can accomplish whatever I put my mind to.*

Sam Moku: *Cool moss! That was great. Everybody on the team did the fire walk, I think, except for one guy. I was pumped up for it. I actually went twice because I wanted to make sure I was doing it right. That was another one of those moments that you look back on and say, "Wow!"*

Joe Onosai: *I was scared as heck! Tony Robbins gave us this motivational talk that lasted about three hours. By the time we got to the hot coals, some of us were ready for it and some of us weren't. I was one of the guys who was just freaking out, not wanting to go. But Nuʻu Faʻaola was the first guy up, and when we saw him walking over the coals like they were nothing, that really gave the rest of us a lot of confidence. Before that, though, the idea of walking over those hot coals scared the daylights out of me.*

Once, I asked Tony, "How do we give ourselves a better chance to beat the likes of Oklahoma and Nebraska?" These perennial powers rarely lost. The Sooners and Cornhuskers would go years without losing to certain teams. A big reason for that was their opponents didn't think they could beat them.

How could we better prepare ourselves mentally to slay these giants?

Tony replied, "Tell your players to close their eyes."

Tony instructed our team to do just that. "I want you to imagine the time in your football careers when you felt the most confident," he'd say. "Think of the time when you most believed in yourself, and when you most believed in your teammates."

The room got real silent. Then Tony continued, "Now, let's transfer this confidence to a game against, say, Oklahoma. If you have this feeling of confidence, do you think you could win? If you do, nod your head."

It was an amazing feeling to see every player nod in agreement. Their breathing changed. The looks on their faces showed complete confidence!

Now, winning is more complicated than that. You can't just be confident and think you're going to win. You must also execute. If you fumble the ball all over the place or miss your assignments, just having confidence isn't going to help.

Tony and I formed a tremendous bond. He told me that a lot of motivational strategies that he liked to share with his audiences were techniques I was already using for my team. These "problem solvers" were psychological and instinctive in nature. The Marathon Encounter that we utilized after our loss to BYU in 1984 is one example. That allowed me to meet every single person on the team, even if it was at an inconvenient time.

We occasionally used other problem-solving techniques, like calling two consecutive time outs to get a point across to the team. After our loss to UTEP in 1980, we used another motivational strategy, "Create a Crisis," after a poor performance. This might include a marathon film session or a Sunday practice at 6:00 a.m., even after a long road trip.

Although rarely used—maybe once every couple of years—these approaches worked more than eighty percent of the time! They were effective ways to alter the trajectory of our season in a positive way.

We benefitted greatly from Tony's methods. The ability to visualize success helped us to perform even better both on and off the field. Through my relationship with Tony, the Rainbow Warriors were able to overcome a lot of challenges.

Except, of course, for beating you-know-who.

While the Rainbow Warriors were never able to score a victory over BYU during my time in Hawai'i, we did set the wheels in motion for that to happen. The lesson we learned here would pay big dividends for the program over the next several years.

Our 10-3 loss to the Cougars during my final season confirmed what our coaching staff had already suspected: We needed to change our offense to better compete with

BYU and other power programs.

At the time, New Mexico had an offensive coordinator named Ben Griffith. Under his tutelage, the Lobos were taking WAC defenses apart with a spread-option attack that typically used four or even five wide receivers. It was still a run-based system, but the spread-option gave offenses the added ability to throw the ball. Paul Johnson was employing a similar style as the offensive coordinator at Georgia Southern.

At the end of the season, Bob Wagner and a couple of other coaches attended the Division I-AA national championship game in Seattle. He witnessed first-hand the effectiveness of the spread-option, as Georgia Southern handily defeated Arkansas State, 48-21. It was the Eagles' second straight national title.

> **Bob Wagner:** *I saw Georgia Southern play, and they were running the spread, which was a blend of the run-and-shoot and triple option. At UH, we were playing power football, and BYU was big and physical enough to handle us. Georgia Southern, I thought, had the answer we were looking for. In the back of my mind, I thought, "Boy, if I ever became a head coach, this is the offense I'd want to run. The spread-option really fascinated me.*

While this was happening, I had no idea that I would be leaving for the University of Arizona. The Wildcats hadn't even approached me yet. When I did go to Arizona, we hired Ben Griffith. Wags, meanwhile, brought in both Paul Johnson and offense line coach Mike Sewak from Georgia Southern.

When Hawai'i changed its offense, I think that changed the entire trajectory of the program. Under Wags, the Rainbow Warriors were able to accomplish things that we couldn't do in my time at Hawai'i, like win the WAC and play in the Holiday Bowl.

And, yes, we finally beat BYU.

We all celebrated the night of October 28, 1989, when Hawai'i finally conquered the Cougars. Announcing the game that night, Jim Leahey kept asking the question, "Could this be the night?" The answer was an emphatic yes!

Final score: UH 56, BYU 14.

> **Rick Blangiardi:** *That was my last game as a TV analyst. I had already moved to the mainland, but I wanted to do that final game against BYU.*
>
> *There had been only a couple of games in all those years where it seemed BYU was just a little too good for us. Other than that, Hawai'i always rose to the occasion. The games were intense. So many times, the crowds at Aloha Stadium would think, "Could this be the year?" only to have BYU pull the rug from under us.*
>
> *So when we finally beat them in 1989, that was sweet. It was a romp, and I left the stadium with such a satisfied feeling. It was a great way to end my ten-plus years*

as an announcer. I still get emotional when I think about it.

In January of 1987, I resigned as the University of Hawai'i head football coach to accept the head coaching position at the University of Arizona.

Larry Smith was in town for the Hula Bowl. Before arriving in Honolulu, it was announced that Larry was leaving Arizona to become the new head coach at USC. After the game, he and I were having lunch, and Larry just said to me, "You know, you ought to look into the Arizona job."

After Larry returned to Arizona, he apparently talked to the school's athletic director, Cedric Dempsey. Cedric, who would later become president of the NCAA, gave me a call.

"If I'm going to do this, I need to do it quickly," I told him. I was concerned for the guys on my coaching staff. If I decided to go to Arizona, I didn't want to leave any of my guys hanging. Also, a protracted process wouldn't be fair to either Hawai'i or Arizona.

It wasn't an easy decision. In fact, I agonized over it for days. There was a point in my deliberations, in fact, that I just couldn't stomach the idea of no longer being in Hawai'i. I loved the Islands and the people. I loved the university and all my coaches and players. I had come to regard Hawai'i as home. Even more importantly, my children, Richie and Angie, also loved it here. They enjoyed being part of a multi-ethnic society.

We had players come to our house all the time. Rich got along with all the guys, while Angie really took to guys like DeWayne Jett, Verlon Redd and Rich Miano. Angie was also close to a couple of neighborhood friends: Lea Woods Almanza is now a noted opera singer, and Devah Pager is a tenured professor at Harvard.

The Arizona job, I knew, was going to be a difficult one. In his seven seasons as the Wildcats' head coach, Larry had only had one losing season. I knew it would be hard to replace a quality guy who was so beloved and successful.

At the same time, there was a lot to like about the Arizona program. I knew that if I ever were to leave Hawai'i, it would have to be for a Pac-10 school on the West Coast and with a warm climate. Arizona checked all those boxes.

I had been a candidate for the Arizona job before, when I was still an assistant at UCLA. I didn't get the position, but I always thought that Arizona was an attractive opportunity.

Finally, I decided it was time for me to take on a new challenge. Opportunities to lead a quality Pac-10 football program didn't come along every day. I needed to do this.

When I returned to Hawai'i from Tucson to break the news to my team, I bawled my eyes out.

Now here's something that I've never made public until now: Less than a week after the news broke that I was in consideration for the Arizona position, I tried to get my job back. The idea of leaving Hawai'i was so traumatizing that I got a severe case of cold feet.

I called our athletic director, Stan Sheriff, and said, "Are you too far along in this process that I can't come back?"

Stan had so much wisdom. He had been a football coach himself, so he knew what I was going through. He could relate to what I was feeling.

Stan just said, "Dick, I'm too far along and you're too far along."

I appreciated Stan for being straight with me and telling me that we were both too far along in the process to turn back. He was a mature individual who had been through the rigors of coaching college football. He understood how much I loved Hawai'i, and he also knew that getting cold feet was oftentimes part of the process. (I had also sought Ray Nagel's advice. Ray told me that if I didn't take the Arizona job, he would never speak to me again!)

And that was it.

> **Bob Wagner:** *When Dick got the Arizona job, I had the opportunity to go with him. He told me that I had a job with him as defensive coordinator if I didn't get the UH [head coaching] job. I was very grateful for Dick for that. It helped ease my mind a bit, and it also gave me a little bit of leverage.*
>
> *Stan Sheriff had a football background, so he understood the game and its challenges. He also knew of my work on defense and special teams, and I was able to talk with him about the kind of offense I wanted to use. I had such a tremendous love affair with the people and culture of Hawai'i—and still do. Getting the opportunity to be a Division I head coach at a school I had special feelings for, well, that was a major goal for me.*

Looking back, I'm happy how everything worked out. It was the perfect situation for everyone involved. I went to Arizona and brought some of my assistants with me. Wags was able to keep some assistants as well as add some of his own guys. I think the program benefits whenever someone on the existing staff gets the head coaching job. It promotes stability and continuity, and it allows the players to maintain a sense of familiarity with their coaches. More often than not, that formula leads to success.

As the familiar saying goes, the rest is history. Wags went on to do a terrific job as head coach of the Rainbow Warriors, taking the program to an even higher level. I moved on to coach at Arizona for fourteen seasons, earning "Pac-10 Coach of the Year" honors in 1992 and finishing as the program's coaching leader in career wins. Later, after stops with the San Francisco 49ers and Texas Longhorns, I returned to the college head coaching ranks, taking the reins of San Jose State's football program for five seasons.

Still, I kept returning to Hawai'i. In 2010, I joined Jim Leahey in the broadcast booth to provide commentary for Rainbow Warrior games. In 2011, I joined Greg McMackin's staff as Hawai'i's special teams coordinator. Even today, I have a connection with Nick Rolovich's Rainbow Warriors team. Rolo's special teams coordinator and defensive ends coach, Mayur Chaudhari, is my son-in-law.

With my departure in 1987, an eventful decade in UH football history had come to a close. The story of the Rainbow Warriors, of course, would continue to grow and extend to destinations and achievements we never before imagined. (Seriously, Hawai'i in the BCS Sugar Bowl?) Each new chapter would reveal its own set of triumphs and disappointments, successes and frustrations.

As the years went on, the legacy of my ten years with the Rainbow Warrior football program would also grow. It expanded in ways I never dreamed of. For example, seven guys on our coaching staffs went on to lead college programs of their own. If you add the future head coaches who served with me at Arizona and San Jose State, that number swells to fourteen (including former Fresno State head coach Pat Hill and former Utah and Weber State head coach Ron McBride. Pat and Ron both served on my coaching staff at Arizona.)

This legacy would, in fact, stretch far beyond the sport of football. Today, it reaches deep into politics, education, business, entertainment and many other vital fields that impact and influence this world we live in.

With that in mind, let's move on to Chapter Nine. You'll see why it's my favorite part of this book.

Chapter Nine

BEYOND THE RAINBOW

Former University of Texas head football coach Mack Brown is a dear friend of mine. I served as his associate head coach in 2004, when the Longhorns went 12-1 and capped the season with a thrilling Rose Bowl win over Michigan.

The next year, I was back in Pasadena to witness Vince Young and the Longhorns beat Reggie Bush and USC for the national crown. I remember the locker room scene after the game. The players and coaches were utterly jubilant. Then, as the celebration began to wind down, Coach Brown stood in front of the group and gave his team one final bit of instruction.

"The job that each of you guys have now," he said, "is that you can't let this be the best thing that ever happened to you."

It was the perfect thing to say.

Successful coaching has to entail more than wins and losses. In fact, as I see it, you could win every single game, claim every possible championship and pack your stadium with fans—if your players are not better people when they finish their college careers than they were when they started, you have failed miserably. As a coach, you have to believe that. If you don't, then you're in the wrong profession.

Your goal as a coach should be to impact your players' lives in a positive way. You need to steer them in a positive direction, and if they veer off course you should do everything you can to bring them back.

In that respect, I view football as a learning laboratory for young people to learn about the adversities of life, and how to handle it all without getting down on themselves. The hope is that your players use football as a means toward a better way forward. You want them to be resourceful with whatever gifts God has given them. Your desire is to see them make the most of their talents both in the classroom and on the field, so when they graduate they can become productive citizens.

If you can do all of that, then coaching is the greatest job in the world.

Of course, no one stays a head coach for very long unless he wins games. That's just the reality of our profession. In my twenty-nine years as a head coach at Hawaiʻi, Arizona and San Jose State, we never had back-to-back losing seasons. The ability to win consistently enabled us to help hundreds of young men both on and off the football field.

As proud as I am of the accomplishments our program made during my time at UH, I am even more proud of the players who have excelled in life after their playing days were over. They have become leaders in their communities and tremendous contributors to our society. They are now fathers and businessmen, public servants and ministers, entertainers and administrators.

"Where Are They Now?" updates of all my former Hawai'i players would be a book by itself. But here are just some of the outstanding alumni who have gone on to achieve great things after their Rainbow Warrior careers.

THE EDUCATOR

Duane Coleman would be the first to tell you that he didn't have the most spectacular UH football career. Although he was a talented and hardworking wide receiver, he didn't score a touchdown for us until the third game of his senior year—a 36-yard reception from Raphel Cherry against Utah.

But in terms of life after football, few people have made an impact quite like Duane, who's been an educator for nearly thirty-five years. Today, he's the superintendent of the Oceanside Unified School District in California. Duane, who grew up in Oceanside, oversees twenty-three schools, more than 2,100 employees and nearly 20,000 students.

Duane isn't someone who simply talks about the importance of a good education. He lives and breathes it. He has two master's degrees (in business and information technology) and a doctorate in educational leadership from Alliant International University.

That's right, he's *Doctor* Duane Coleman. Here's his story on how he turned a personal tragedy into a devoted calling.

> **Duane Coleman:** *I'll be honest with you: Education wasn't my biggest priority at UH. I was more focused on football and getting to the NFL. But I did make sure I got my degree because I didn't want to be someone who went to college and didn't finish.*
>
> *In my senior year, I had a daughter, Jade. Afterward, I was with the Denver Broncos for a year, but I blew out my knee. I needed to get a job. In 1984, several months after returning to Oceanside, I lost my daughter to Sudden Infant Death Syndrome (SIDS). Losing her was the catalyst for just about everything I do in my life now.*
>
> *Today, I try to pay attention to every single student. I know that's physically impossible, but I can't afford to not do whatever I can for every single student. I owe it to them. I love this city so much. I'm willing to give it my best, and I expect everyone else to be giving their best, or they shouldn't be working here. I don't want anything but the best for Oceanside. We have gang issues here, and it's getting to the*

point where [gang-related deaths] happen at least once a month. I don't want us to get used to that. I believe that the only way to change that is through education.

Coach Tomey always stressed to us the importance of hard work and preparation. He told us, "You're going to work hard, know your plays and make good decisions." Those are the kinds of lessons that paid off for me, and today we try to pass them on to our students.

THE ENTREPRENEUR

Pat Schmidt was our starting free safety during my first year in Hawai'i, in 1977. Although the senior transfer from UCLA only played one season at UH, he certainly was a key contributor to our team. Pat was known for his ferocious, bone-crunching hits that you could hear from the top of Aloha Stadium.

After leaving Hawai'i, Pat got a free agent tryout with the Los Angeles Rams and later played for the USFL's Chicago Blitz. He got into coaching for a while, taking over the sophomore team at West Torrance High School in California, his alma mater. Then, as he says, "God called me in a different direction."

In 1988, Pat founded FFF Enterprises, widely regarded as the country's leading supplier of critical care biopharmaceuticals, plasma products and vaccines. This California-based company does nearly $2 billion in annual sales and serves over eighty percent of all hospitals in the United States.

Obviously, Pat's contributions in the field of medicine have been even more impactful than the hits he made as a football player.

Pat Schmidt: *I found the transition from football coach to CEO to be pretty easy. There are four quarters in business, just as there are four quarters in football. At the end of the year, you either made money or lost money; you won the game or lost the game.*

In football, a head coach leads lots of different types of personnel. There are big guys and small guys, people that throw and people that catch. A football team is a very diverse organization in terms of the different skill sets that are required. Business is exactly the same way. You have sales people and accounting people and legal people. Each group has a different skill set. The job of a CEO is just like the job of a head coach: You have to get each person into the position that will help the team the most.

THE ADMINISTRATOR

I can't say enough good things about Blane Gaison. He was such a great leader for us. One of the things I always looked for in a player was attitude. I wanted guys who were serious about being good, and dead serious about being part of a winning team. Blane was one of those guys. He was just a winner. He wanted to learn. He went to all the meetings. He had a maniacal workout regimen that he put himself through. Blane did things the right way.

His work ethic certainly paid off. After graduating from UH, Blane spent four years as a safety for the Atlanta Falcons. When his playing days were done, he returned to his alma mater, Kamehameha Schools-Kapālama, and served as the school's head coach and athletic director. He later became the athletic director at Kamehameha Schools' Maui campus.

In October of 2015, Blane was named the new executive director for the Interscholastic League of Honolulu (ILH). His position allows him to further his lifelong mission to help Hawai'i's young people.

> **Blane Gaison:** *You're talking about a kid who grew up in the streets of Kalihi. I was able to fulfill a dream that I never before could have imagined. I played in the NFL because of the University of Hawai'i football program and because of coaches like Coach Tomey, who gave me the opportunity to develop my skills and my ability to reach that high level.*
>
> *Today, as executive director of the ILH, I get to assist the young people who are in our interscholastic sports programs and hopefully give them that hope and faith that they can achieve all the things I did. I'm trying to pay it forward and pass on what I learned from my coaches. The message is, "Hey, you too can live that dream. You too can have that success. It's just a matter of knowing what needs to be done and knowing how to do it."*

THE PASTOR

What happens when your dream of playing in the NFL is suddenly shattered? Joe Onosai, an outstanding offensive lineman for us from 1983 to 1986, faced that setback. One minute, he was a rookie in the Dallas Cowboys huddle, alongside the likes of Tony Dorsett and Herschel Walker. The next minute, he was on a stretcher, unable to move. The spinal injury was severe enough to end Joe's pro football aspirations.

Fortunately, Joe's story didn't end there. He rebuilt himself physically, mentally and emotionally. In fact, in 1994 he was a finalist in the World's Strongest Man Competition, a feat he repeated the following year. His new career as a strongman took him all over the world, including stops in the Bahamas, Malta, Germany, Scotland and Sweden.

Today, Joe is the senior pastor at Destiny Christian Church in Pearl City. He recently came out with a book, *The Power of Destiny: The Journey of Discovering My Purpose*, which details his inspiring life journey.

> **Joe Onosai:** *I thought my destiny was to play in the NFL. Ever since I was a kid, it just seemed that everything was pointed in that direction. So when the door was suddenly shut, I was confused and hurt. I fell into a major depression. But now*

I can share my life from the perspective of, "This is where I was." Yes, I've experienced disappointment. But I'm so grateful that things turned out for the better.

I live with such a grateful heart. In hindsight, you can see the hand of God in my life. Things didn't work out the way I thought they would, but if you were to ask me if I would change anything, I would say no. Even with all the pain and hurt that I've been through, I've learned so much.

And I learned so much from Coach Tomey. His saying that's forever ingrained in me is, "I'd rather you be consistently good than occasionally great." I was very consistent in football but not very consistent off the field. I think that challenged me to want to be better off the field. He made such a difference in my life, in helping me take the passion I had in football and put it into my family life. He definitely made an impact on my life.

THE PERFORMER

Greg Cummins was one of the best punters we ever had at UH. His 40.66-yard punting average still places him in the top ten among all Rainbow Warrior punters. In 1977 he booted a 73-yard beauty for us against Colorado State!

Greg is still getting his kicks in, but now it's as a Hollywood actor. Gregory Scott Cummins has appeared in numerous TV series, including *Murphy Brown, Walker, Texas Ranger, Baywatch, Buffy the Vampire Slayer* and *NCIS*. On the big screen, you've seen Greg in the Sylvester Stallone flick *Cliffhanger* and in *Batman Returns*. Currently, he has recurring roles on the TV series *It's Always Sunny in Philadelphia* and *Bosch*.

While he was at UH, Greg had the benefit of studying under the great Terence Knapp, a noted actor and educator who was the university's Emeritus Professor of Theatre.

Greg Cummins: *In spring ball before my senior season, I had the lead in Shakespeare's* As You Like It. *Opening night was the same night as our alumni game. Coach Tomey just said, "That's fine." He completely let me go and do that. I was shocked. Coach supported me taking drama when, in those days, coaches didn't really care about that kind of thing. They cared more about football. But Coach Tomey cared about my education, and I've never forgotten that.*

Coach Tomey cared about us as individuals. He cared more about what we were going to do with the rest of our lives than he did about winning. That's why we played so hard for him. The entire coaching staff had that attitude.

Coach created such a great team atmosphere. We didn't have guys fighting over starting positions. Even if you didn't get a starting position, you rooted for the guys who did. I think we played way over our heads those first couple of years because we were really bonded to each other. I've carried the "team" aspect into my professional life. The concept of teamwork works in every phase of life, whether it's the entertainment industry or the business world. It's about caring about people and creating unity.

I've been doing this for thirty-three years now. I'm not a big star or anything, but I can say that I made a living for thirty-three years as a professional actor, and I'm proud of that.

THE PROTECTOR

Sam Tong was a defensive lineman who played for three UH head coaches: Dave Holmes, Larry Price and yours truly. He played alongside some of the finest lineman in the history of our program, including Levi Stanley, John Woodcock, Cliff Laboy, Tom Tuinei and Harris Matsushima.

After his time as a Rainbow Warrior, Sam joined the United States Secret Service. Talk about interesting transitions—Sam went from stuffing running backs to protecting U.S. presidents!

Sam served with the Secret Service for more than twenty-five years, eventually heading the agency's Honolulu office. His four and a half years of presidential protection duty including providing security for presidents Ronald Reagan and George H.W. Bush. In addition, he was assigned to protect Bill Clinton during his presidential run in 1992.

In June 1987, when President Reagan made his famous, "Mr. Gorbachev, tear down this wall!" speech in front of the Brandenburg Gate in West Berlin, Sam was there, watching the proceedings from one side of the stage.

Sam Tong: *As a local boy growing up in Kāne'ohe, I loved reading about all the different places in the world. But they were just pictures in a social studies book. I never imagined that I would one day be able to go to these places and actually see them.*

It was an incredible experience being in the Secret Service and dealing with different people all over the world, learning what their cultural differences were and working within that framework. We had to work with the local governments, police agencies and embassies to get the job done. We weren't just agents; we were also ambassadors and diplomats. We were representing our country as well as our organization.

Playing football at UH helped me prepare for those challenges. We learned to overcome adversity and find solutions to problems. Being able to adjust and be flexible are important skills in any field of work. The guys I played with all had that certain mental toughness. They're fighters. They were always figuring out how to compensate for their weaknesses and to emphasize their strengths. They were always finding ways to solve problems. I think that's the biggest thing that you learn from playing sports.

THE MAYOR

Bernard Carvalho may be the ultimate "local boy makes good" story. We recruited Bernard out of Kapaʻa High School on the island of Kauaʻi. From 1979 to 1983, he was a dependable anchor on our offensive line and later played for the NFL's Miami Dolphins.

After football, Bernard returned to Kauaʻi to serve his community. In 2002, he was appointed director of the Office of Community Assistance, overseeing several Kauaʻi County agencies including transportation, housing, recreation and the elderly. In 2008, he was elected mayor of Kauaʻi County in a special election to replace Bryan Baptiste, who died in office. Bernard subsequently was reelected to four-year terms in 2010 and 2014.

I should have known that Bernard was destined for politics. At Kapaʻa High School, he served as student body president. I just think it's a wonderful example of a young man doing everything he could in football, and then returning home to serve his community.

Bernard Carvalho: Coach Tomey had this way of inspiring us and always giving us hope. We never gave up. I remember one time after a big loss, there were arrows posted all over the bathroom and everywhere we went. The arrows were all pointing upward. We thought, "What is this? What does this mean?" Coach told us that it was a visual reminder for us to keep looking up and keep going forward.

I'm always using football terminology in what I do today. I incorporate what I learned in football in everything that we do. I'll tell one of my department heads, "You know what? You're sitting on the bench. I'm calling in this other guy." Or I'll say, "The people of Kauaʻi are sitting in the stands watching us, and we're doing nothing. Come on, guys, put on your chinstraps!"

Sometimes I tell my guys, "We're on the 10-yard line, but a field goal is not acceptable. We're going for the touchdown on this one!" When you do that, it gets everybody pumped and in "Let's go!" mode.

What I learned from Coach Tomey is that it doesn't matter how big or small you are. What matters is your heart. If you have a strong heart and faith, then anything is possible.

THE UNDERDOG

I'll say this right up front: I could not possibly be prouder of Pete Noga. Here's a guy who came from humble beginnings to achieve greatness both on and off the football field. Pete emerged from the lengthy shadows of his brothers Niko and Al to create a wonderful life for himself and his lovely bride, Taunuʻu Veʻe-Noga. (Taunuʻu is herself quite a success story. She's in the process of earning a doctoral degree at the University of the Pacific.)

Pete was a terrific linebacker for us from 1982 through 1986. The next year, he earned a spot with the NFL's St. Louis Cardinals, playing alongside his older brother, Niko. Against the Washington Redskins that season, Pete intercepted a pass and raced 60 yards for a touchdown.

To me, Pete is a perfect example of every lesson I tried to impart to my players. His life has always been about overcoming obstacles, working hard and being persistent.

Pete Noga: *I grew up in Kalihi. To earn a full football scholarship and attend the University of Hawai'i, that was a huge challenge for me. But I faced it head-on. I was never afraid of challenges. I was never afraid of learning and asking questions.*

Man, it's been thirty years since my time at UH. It seems just like yesterday. I learned a lot from Coach Tomey. He was a very straight person who taught me to be a good player and a good person. He was both a teacher and a mentor.

After football, I wanted to continue working in the community. I was a sheriff for a time. I wanted to work in law enforcement to help out our youth. Then I became a driver for Teamsters Local 399 in Hollywood. I even did some acting and stunt work. In fact, if I'd pursued a career as a stunt man, I think I would have been one of the best. The coordinator told me, "Hey, Noga, you're a natural!"

Today, I'm loving life in the Bay Area with my beautiful wife, Taunu'u.

Being part of the Noga legacy really humbles me. Our legacy really began with my mom and dad. Everything we have, we owe to them, to our Heavenly Father and to all our uncles, aunties and friends who played a part in our lives. It's amazing, but we still have so many fans. I walk down the street and people will come up to me and say, "Thank you for what you've done."

THE COACHES

As I previously mentioned, fourteen of my assistant coaches went on to lead their own college football programs. One of them is Dino Babers, who played safety, linebacker and running back for the Rainbow Warriors from 1979 to 1983. Dino later served as a graduate assistant for us at Hawai'i, then continued to build his résumé at various schools until rejoining me at Arizona in 1995. In 1998, I promoted Dino to offensive coordinator and quarterbacks coach. He would later become head coach at Eastern Illinois (where his quarterback was Jimmy Garoppolo) and Bowling Green.

In December 2015, Dino was named head coach of the Syracuse Orange. His first year with the program including a memorable upset victory over Virginia Tech. (Go to YouTube and search "Syracuse Postgame Locker Room" to see why his players love Dino so much.)

As a player, Kenny Niumatalolo is primarily regarded as Garrett Gabriel's backup quarterback during the early years of Bob Wagner's tenure. Few people remember that Kenny actually joined our program in 1983 before going on a two-year church mission.

Kenny became a disciple of Paul Johnson's spread option offense, following Paul to the Naval Academy in 1995. In December 2007, he was promoted to head coach of the Midshipmen and hasn't looked back since. In 2008, Navy upset No. 16 Wake Forest to claim the program's first win over a ranked team in twenty-three years. Under Kenny's leadership, Navy has beaten Notre Dame three times. Most important of all, of course, the Midshipmen were 9-0 against rival Army in Kenny's first nine seasons.

Dino and Kenny are two of the finest "youngish" coaches in college football, and I couldn't be more proud of them.

Dino Babers: *Oh, my goodness, I loved Hawai'i. To this day, when I hear "Hawai'i Five-O," it makes the hair stand up on my arms!*

I knew I wanted to be a coach when I first got into college. That's one of the reasons why I was so eager and willing to switch positions whenever they asked me. I wanted to be coached by different personalities and teachers so that I could take the best part from each coach.

The one thing we talk about all the time here at Syracuse is that we're a family. We're la familia. We're 'ohana. Of course, I had to explain to the guys what "'ohana" is. So, yes, we're teaching some Hawaiian words out here on the East Coast!

Kenny Niumatalolo: *You know, I didn't realize it then, but many of the things that I learned from Coach Tomey are the things that I carry on today. For example, Coach emphasized ball security. I remember doing these monkey roll drills, with three guys jumping over each other with the ball. When you hit the ground, you had to make sure the ball was secure under your shoulder. It was hard because your first instinct was to use your hands to brace yourself when you hit the ground. But today at Navy, we rank pretty high in the country in terms of ball security. I'm a stickler on it, and I got that from Coach Tomey.*

THE CHAMPION

In football, is there a Rainbow Warrior alumnus who is as accomplished as Jesse Sapolu? Born in Samoa, the former Farrington High School standout played fifteen seasons in the NFL, all with the San Francisco 49ers. He was a fixture on the Niners' impenetrable offensive line and was twice named All-Pro. Most impressively, Jesse helped San Francisco win four Super Bowl titles (1985, 1989, 1990 and 1995).

He achieved it all despite living with a life-threatening heart condition, a story that he recounts in his 2012 memoir, *I Left My Heart in San Francisco*.

Today, Jesse remains active with the 49ers, doing community relations work for the team. He is also one of the founders of the Polynesian Football Hall of Fame, an organization of which I am proud to be a part. In 2015, Jesse himself was inducted into the Hall.

Jesse Sapolu: *Coach Tomey was one of the toughest coaches you could ever play for. Now, there are two ways you can look at it. One, you can leave the program because you can't handle it. Or, two, you can embrace it, overcome it and become a tough football player.*

When I joined the 49ers, as the practices got longer and harder, I would hear other guys grumble. They'd complain, "Man, this is ridiculous!" But I was actually enjoying it. I was used to tough practices. So Coach Tomey teaching me toughness and never taking the easy way out really helped me in my NFL career.

THE FINANCIER

Larry Goeas was a linebacker and defensive lineman for us during my early years in Hawai'i. He was one of those guys who worked for everything he got. We didn't recruit him. Instead, he recruited us. He just called me one day in 1978 and asked for an opportunity to be a Rainbow Warrior.

Larry's one of the great rags-to-riches stories in the history of UH football. Not only did he earn a spot on our team, he was selected as our Most Valuable Defensive Scout that season. He was named co-Warrior of the Year in 1980, sharing the honor with Niko Noga. The following season, he won the award outright.

Today, Larry works as hard as ever, but now he works to help people secure their financial futures. He is the senior vice president and branch manager of Raymond James, one of the top wealth management firms in the country.

Larry Goeas: *In February of 1983, I was planning to play in the USFL. Doug Kay had left UH to take over the defense of the Boston Breakers, and he invited me to try out for the team.*

But Coach Tomey found out that I also had a job offer from American Express. Dick called me into his office. He said, "Larry, I have no doubt that you could make it with the Boston Breakers. But it's going to be a struggle. You might play two or three years, maybe four. But when it's all over, you're going to have to come back and start a career. I strongly advise you to take this job offer and leave football alone."

Man, for the first couple of years, I regretted [passing on football] so much. I missed the game. But after the third or fourth year, I realized that it was the right decision. I had clients like Jesse Sapolu, Mark Tuinei and Ma'a Tanuvasa. Years later, I told Dick, "That was the best advice anybody ever gave me." He really was looking out for me.

I love what I do. I went through the 1987 [stock market] crash and the 2008 crash. Those are the times when you learn what kind of consultant you are. That's when you can really help people. When the tough times come, I just go back to the lessons I learned as a University of Hawai'i player. You just keep on working hard.

THE VISIONARY

Marco Johnson's story is nothing short of remarkable. After graduating from UH, the former Rainbow Warrior running back and wide receiver returned home to Los Angeles and became a firefighter and paramedic. In 1997, after witnessing too many unnecessary deaths, Marco began offering CPR and first aid classes to the public. Within twelve years, he and his wife Sandra turned that endeavor into the University of Antelope Valley (UAV), a regionally accredited institution offering associate, bachelor's and master's degrees in a variety of programs.

Today, as founder and president of UAV, Marco continues to serve his hometown as a leading proponent of higher education.

Marco Johnson: *My wife got tired of me coming home and complaining about how I wish someone would have started CPR/first aid before we arrived on the scene. She just said, "Stop complaining and do something about it." That's how it all began.*

Fast forward five or six years, and we started looking at private institutions and how they were born. USC was founded by a group of businessmen who decided to make it happen. San Diego State was founded by a pharmacist who started with a pharmacy tech program. Georgetown repurposed a ton of old properties and created their university. So we studied the approaches they took and mimicked them. We repurposed an old hotel, the Antelope Valley Inn, by gutting many of the guest rooms and converting them into classrooms. We also kept between sixty-five and 100 of the rooms and turned them into on-campus housing. We later introduced athletics and a ton of campus clubs for extracurricular activities. We essentially evolved into a traditional four-year university.

It's absolutely a blessing. It's mind blowing. It seems somewhat surreal that this is really happening. I do think that my experiences in Hawai'i gave me an attitude of aloha that I was able to bring back with me to Antelope Valley. The aloha spirit I experienced in Hawai'i built a sense of me needing to give back to my community.

THE SERVANT

I still kid Sam Moku about our 1984 victory over San Diego State. That's the game where Sam got ejected for fighting with the Aztecs' star receiver, Webster Slaughter. Because Slaughter also got ejected, we thought we got the better end of that deal. After the game, I pointed to Sam and told the team, "Everybody can contribute in different ways."

Today Sam is still contributing, but in a far larger way. He has served the Hawai'i community through both the state and Honolulu city governments. Over the years, Sam worked at the State Legislature, Department of Hawaiian Home Lands and at City Hall under then-Mayor Peter Carlisle. In 2013, he joined Hawai'i Pacific

University as director of public and governmental relations. He was later named the school's vice president of university relations.

In 2015, *Hawaii Business* magazine named Sam as one of "20 for the Next 20"—a designation given to local leaders "whose talents, accomplishments and potential set them apart as emerging leaders of Hawai'i into the next two decades."

If you ask me, they could not have made a better selection.

Sam Moku: *For me, I always go back to the theme of hard work. You might not be able to control how big you are or how tall you are, but you can control how hard you work. My mom and dad weren't athletes, but growing up I always liked to run and be in shape. I just had the desire to work hard and be my best, and I think that carried over in my life.*

One of my mentors in my UH days was Blane Gaison. When I was in high school, I would see him doing his workouts, and after he left I would go and mimic the same workout. After that, we kind of built a bond.

When Peter Carlisle was mayor, I was appointed as his director of community service. I was trying to build team camaraderie among my staff, which numbered about 300 at the time. So I arranged for a strategic planning meeting with Coach Tomey as the guest speaker. Coach came in, and he was great! Most of my staff knew all about Coach Tomey, and he helped me to galvanize my staff to buy into my strategic plan.

THE INSPIRATION

Tom Tuinei was a fabulous defensive lineman for us from 1976 to 1979, but that's not why he's included in this chapter. Tom went on to have a productive professional career in both the NFL and CFL, but, again, his football résumé is not the reason why I'm mentioning him now.

Born to a Samoan father and Czechoslovakian mother, Tom grew up in Wai'anae and was recruited to UH by defensive line coach Charlie Ka'aihue. He was big, fast and strong as a bull. He was an amazing athlete. However, like many other young people, he had some issues. He needed structure. He needed a support system. We did our best to provide him with those things, but Tom went through some really difficult times.

I'll let him take it from here:

Tom Tuinei: *I started getting involved with drugs. I started to rip people off. Instead of doing positive things with my talent, I began to do bad things. I got in trouble for ripping off some drug dealers to support my habit. I finally got caught and was handed a twenty-year prison sentence, but I wound up serving the mandatory five at Hālawa. This was way back in 1990.*

After that, I knew I had to get my act together. Only a stupid guy would go back to prison.

My younger brother Mark passed away in 1999. Being two years older, I was sort of a role model for him. He followed what I did. Football was my thing, and it became his thing. But Mark made a mistake, too, and it cost him his life. I should have done more for Mark. That's one of my real regrets. I wish I was a better role model for him. (Mark Tuinei, who played for us in 1982, was a Pro Bowl offensive lineman for the Dallas Cowboys. He helped his team capture three Super Bowl championships. In May of 1999, Mark died of a drug overdose.)

Today, I talk to young people about following their dreams and making the right choices in life. I make a short presentation, show them some football memorabilia and then speak to them about not giving up on life. It's no secret that ice is an epidemic here in Hawai'i. It caught me, too. The majority of people who use it go down, and I don't want others to make the mistakes I did.

You know, most of the people in prison are really talented people. I know that sounds funny to say, but they are. In prison, most of them are sober, and you can see their talents. They're healthy and they're thinking straight. It's the alcohol and drugs that destroy them.

I paid my debt to society, and God has blessed me and helped me. I have a great job now, and it feels good to be able to support my family.

Honestly, I just hope I can make a difference. I don't get paid for speaking to the youth. I just want to do it. Only time will tell how many lives I've touched, but hopefully the kids I talk to will grasp what I'm trying to say.

My son Tumua is now playing for UH. In fact, about a year ago he came home and told me that he switched his jersey number to 88, my old number. To me, that's the ultimate sign of respect and love. He just said, "Dad, this is the number I'm going to wear now." It really touched me. I smile whenever I see him hustling on the field. It just feels good.

One day, I was watching a UH practice with Tom when Tumua came running over. Tom introduced me to his son. In front of Tumua, Tom turned to me and said, "I'm so proud of him. He's a better person than I was when I was his age." It was heartwarming to see Tom finally proud of himself!

Tom could have given up on himself, but he didn't. His life represents the ultimate comeback story. It just goes to show that in life, just like in football, there are victories and setbacks. There are hills and valleys. But as my old college professor might remind me, we grow the most when we find ourselves in the deepest of valleys.

Tom Tuinei is a wonderful example of that. ❦

Chapter Ten

CAN IT BE DONE AGAIN?

SEPTEMBER 3, 1998. THE ASHEN CLOUDS that lingered over Aloha Stadium reflected my disposition as I began my retreat to the visitors' locker room. Although I was happy for the win, I took no joy in beating my former team. All around me, Arizona Wildcat players were reveling in the convincing 27-6 season-opening victory. For the Wildcats, it was the start of a remarkable season—a campaign that saw us finish 12-1, including a Holiday Bowl triumph over Nebraska. We would finish No. 4 in the country.

For Hawai'i, it was the first setback of what would turn out to be a winless season for the Rainbow Warriors. Their head coach, Fred von Appen, would be dismissed at the end of the year.

"Coach!"

I turned to see who had called me, and there he was.

Gary Allen.

I hadn't seen Gary in a long while. He was at the game as the latest inductee into the UH Sports Circle of Honor.

He ran over to me, and we embraced. I held him tight. It was so good to see Gary again. I didn't want to let go.

When you have so many fond memories of such a special time in your life, it's always hard to let go.

As I'm writing this, it's June 2017. I'm reminded that, around this time forty years ago, I was hired as the University of Hawai'i's head football coach. I had no idea then that the next ten years would have such an indelible impact on me and the Rainbow Warrior program.

We achieved a lot in those ten years. We joined the Western Athletic Conference. We earned the first national ranking in our program's history. We set attendance records that may never be broken. We challenged—and beat—some of the nation's perennial football powerhouses.

When I first joined the UH program, I viewed my head coaching position as a job. In short order, however, it became much more than that. It became a cause.

We were determined to make this little speck in the middle of the Pacific something special in intercollegiate athletics. Les Murakami and Dave Shoji were already doing it for baseball and volleyball, but it had not yet happened for football. That was the challenge. That was the cause that the coaches, players, support staff and administration all embraced. Most important of all, the people of Hawaiʻi adopted this cause.

Everything we accomplished, we accomplished together, as ʻohana.

I get this question a lot: Can it be done again?

The query isn't about duplicating our on-field successes. As I've said many times, Rainbow Warrior football doesn't begin and end with Dick Tomey. Not even close. I don't have to tell you that my successor, Bob Wagner, elevated the UH program to even greater heights. Under Wags, Hawaiʻi captured the WAC championship, beat Illinois in the Holiday Bowl and lifted the BYU curse. A few years later, June Jones took the program to a larger national stage. His 2007 team went a spotless 12-0 in the regular season and earned a coveted BCS Sugar Bowl appearance. June's successor, Greg McMackin, also won a conference title and led the Rainbow Warriors to a pair of postseason appearances.

What's disappointing to me is that the departures of all three of these head coaches—Wags, June and Mack—were so horribly bungled by the school's administrations at the time. I understand that sometimes a coaching change might be needed or desired—when I was at Arizona, some angry fans even started a Web site called "FireDickTomey.com"—but these partings should be done with class and dignity. Instead, the departures of Wags, June and Mack were awkward at best and ugly at worst. My hope is that the current leaders at the university can learn from those past episodes, and I suspect that they will.

My time at UH was more than wins and losses. It was also about capturing the hearts of the Hawaiʻi fans and building a swell of community support that allowed Hawaiʻi football to become, at the time, the hottest ticket in town. It was about Aloha Stadium filled all the way up into the yellow section, with rabid fans living and dying by the Rainbow Warriors.

With University of Hawaiʻi football, it's not a matter of being great again. With the right people in charge, we know the program will always enjoy periods of success. And in my estimation, with head coach Nick Rolovich and athletic director David Matlin leading the way, the program is heading in the right direction.

The question is, can Rainbow Warrior football be special again?

The answer is, maybe.

Blane Gaison: *I'd love to see it happen again, but I don't know. Times have* *changed. Kids today have so many other options. There are so many other things that people can do for entertainment. Back in our day, there was really only one choice for the weekend, and that was to go to a University of Hawai'i football game.*

I'd like to hope that they can do it. Nick Rolovich has a connection to UH, and the community can relate to him. I'm keeping my fingers crossed because he did a great job [in 2016], and I hope people will come back and buy into the Rainbow Warrior program again.

Bob Wagner: *There are a lot of variables involved. Now, there are so many games that you can watch on TV, including UH. You can bring friends over to your house, have a tailgate party and watch Hawai'i play on TV. Also, the stadium is older and the ticket prices have gone up. Plus, when the old WAC dissolved, it just wasn't the same league.*

Jesse Sapolu: *People today don't have as much appreciation for things like UH football. Back in the day, we'd have to physically go to the library to look up something or study a subject. Now, you get what you want with just a push of a button. I used to watch Joe Moore or Les Keiter doing the nightly sportscasts. You didn't want to fall asleep because you wanted to catch those last seven minutes of the local news because you wanted to watch sports. Today, you just turn on ESPN at any time or press a button on your computer and you'll find every score there is. There's no longer that hunger or excitement of finding out what's going on because everything's so easy now.*

David Toloumu: *I think that Rolo's bringing the camaraderie back. Being a former Rainbow Warrior himself, he knows what it's all about. The guys he has now really believe in each other and play for each other. I attended a practice last year, the week they played Tennessee Martin. I could feel some electricity on that field. It was cool because Rolo let us be on the field and talk to all the guys.*

I would like to think that the perfect storm that created our particular era of UH football can be repeated, but there are many obstacles that must be overcome. Certainly, pay-per-view has had a negative impact on home attendance. The advent of conference championship games means that the big schools no longer have the luxury of making a late-season appearance in the Islands. And as others have pointed out, there are just so many other entertainment options out there, from Facebook and Netflix to YouTube and video games.

UH football needs to be important again. Every game should be a "happening." If the football program can find a way to once more ignite the passion of the fans and bring them to the games in large numbers, maybe then the magic can be rekindled.

I'm rooting for it to happen. I'd love to see a whole new generation of Rainbow Warrior fans celebrate "Saturday night fever" at Aloha Stadium. I'd love for our fans to once again feel the electricity and excitement that we experienced together during my time coaching Rainbow Warrior football.

Forty years ago, when I was a candidate for the vacant head coaching position at the University of Hawai'i, a friend and colleague pulled me aside and said, "You don't want this, Dick."

But I did. And I'm so glad that I did!

Coaching the Rainbow Warriors was one of the greatest experiences of my life. That entire decade that we all shared together—every coach, every player, every fan—is a time that I will always cherish. It was special. It was magic.

It was unforgettable.

ACKNOWLEDGMENTS

I WOULD LIKE TO THANK my former wife, Mary Tomey, and our children, Rich and Angie, who came to love these Islands and still do, and who sacrificed in ways big and small. Rich, Angie and I agree that the greatest gift of living here was to live in a multicultural environment. We will never again come to these shores and feel like strangers. We will always feel like *kamaʻaina*.

I would also like to acknowledge every player, coach and member of the UH football support staff who contributed to our program during my time as head coach of the Rainbow Warriors. Being part of a major college football team requires an incredible amount of commitment, dedication, hard work and selflessness. I wish I could name every one of you individually, but that is not possible. Just know that your contributions are greatly appreciated.

If it were possible, I would also list every family member, player, coach and friend who contributed in some way to the final product that you now hold in your hands. Due to space limitations, however, I will confine myself to those who assisted in the actual process of making this book happen.

Outside of my family, the greatest support for this project came from aio founder and CEO Duane Kurisu, whose encouragement was steady and unwavering. Also, I would have been lost without the expert guidance of George Engebretson, publisher of Watermark Publishing. This book was a tremendous undertaking, and George was the person who pulled it all together.

Lance Tominaga, my co-writer, was a difference maker who helped this first-time author organize his thoughts and anecdotes. Together, Lance and I interviewed more than 150 former UH players, coaches and fans. As conflicts arose, we agreed to be able to disagree and tell the truth as we saw it. We had several key moments that allowed this project to have substance and clarity, insight and reality.

Dave Heenan is a close friend of mine who happens to be a terrific writer as well. Dave was instrumental in giving me the confidence that this project was well worth doing. (Dave, you were right!)

Neal Iwamoto of the University of Hawaiʻi Sports Media Relations Department was invaluable in sorting through the many files, photos, articles, media guides and game programs that helped us attain the information we needed. Mahalo also to UH athletic director David Matlin, who generously provided us access to that information.

I also want to thank the *Honolulu Star-Advertiser* for assistance in securing some of the photos in this book.

I think one of the best examples of collaboration was with Kenny Niumatalolo, who is one of the best head football coaches in the country. Kenny, Lance and I tossed around ideas for the Foreword, which ended up being a product of Kenny's unique perspective as a former UH player and coach—and as a lifelong Rainbow Warrior fan.

We built a team that worked well together and knew their business. We hope you enjoy the final result.

INDEX

A

Acosta, Bob 22, 29, 42
Adams, Theo 96
Afalava, Kesi 52, 70, 116, 124
Aguilar, David 85, 96 *See also* Dyas, David
Ah Yuen, Keith 59, 82
Ainge, Danny 91
Akeo, Ladd 99
Akina, Duane 63, 106
Akiu, Mike 95
Alexander, Robert 72, 81
Allen, Gary ix, 4, 34, 56, 62, 63, 68, 70, 71, 72, 82, 91, 93, 94, 103, 109, 144
Allen, Marcus 64, 66
Almadova, Bryan 52
Almanza, Lea Wood 128
Amosa, Amosa 52
Anae, Robert 99
Arnold, Larry 7
Arnsparger, Bill 10
Arslanian, Dave 31
Arslanian, Sark 30, 31
Arvanetis, Mike 43, 66
Asato, Jimmy 7
Asmus, Jim 70, 80, 81, 92, 103
Atwood, Mike 44

B

Babers, Dino 38, 83, 106, 109, 123, 138
Baker, Noland 82
Baldwin, Tony 23
Balholm, Neil 93
Baptiste, Bryan 137
Bass, Ron "Sunshine" 47
Beazley, Michael 52, 84
Bell, George 29, 32, 41, 44, 45, 47, 48, 56, 72
Bell, Ricky 66
Black, Wayne 66, 69
Blangiardi, Rick 88, 89, 102, 108, 110, 127
Bosco, Robbie 96, 100
Botelho, Don "Spud" 7
Bradley, Danny 85
Brady, Kerry 85
Bray, Fr. Kenneth A. 16
Breland, Jeff 109
Brennan, Colt 61, 107
Briggs, Walter 88
Brostek, Bern 61
Brown, Mack 63, 131
Brown, Paul 10
Brown, Ron 70
Buchanan, Tim 7
Buck, Jack 50
Budde, Brad 66
Burns, John A. 108
Burt, Bob 18, 19, 51, 58
Bush, Fred 87
Bush, George H.W. 136

Bush, Reggie 131
Buss, Jerry 111

C

Cabral, Jeff 23, 29, 31, 69
Capers, Dom 44
Carlen, Jim 46, 47, 82
Carlisle, Peter 141, 142
Carter, Gary 51
Carter, Michael 57
Carvalho, Bernard 38, 82, 137
Case, Scott 85
Castro, Nick 38
Chaudhari, Mayur 130
Cherry, Jerri 86
Cherry, Raphael "Ralph" 84, 85–86, 95, 105, 117, 132
Chow, Norm 99
Clark, Nicky 69
Clark, Tom 23, 32, 66
Clinton, Bill 136
Coleman, Duane 38, 132
Coleman, Jade 132
Coleman, Tim 58
Collins, Bobby 42
Coloma, Burton 30, 35, 45, 47, 56, 67, 69
Cooper, John 12
Coryell, Don 17
Coury, Dick 14
Craig, Roger 64, 76, 83, 84
Cross, Randy 2
Crowell, Danny 88, 118
Culp, Curley 69
Cummins, Greg 30, 47, 49, 67, 69, 135
Cunningham, Randall 99

D

Daniels, Bill 111
Davis, Anthony 66
Davis, Darrell "Mouse" 43

Dempsey, Cedric 128
De Niro, Robert 111
Derby, Brian 64, 65, 85, 86, 96, 97, 104, 106, 116, 121
Donahue, Terry 2, 12, 13, 22, 82
Donovan, Jim 82
Dorazio, Dan 18, 20
Dorsett, Tony 134
Duva, Jeff 22, 24, 29–31, 37, 41, 45, 47, 66, 67–68
Dyas, David 88 *See also* Aguilar, David

E

Easley, Kenny 23
Edgar, Anthony 62, 82, 93, 94, 95
Edra, Fialele 43
Edralin, Daryl 45, 62
Edwards, Lavell 91, 92, 96, 99
Ellerson, Rich 18, 60, 107, 108
Elliott, John "Jumbo" 89
Ellison, Riki *See* Gray, Riki
Ewbank, Weeb 10

F

Faʻaola, Nuʻu 62, 65, 95, 96, 103, 111, 124, 125
Fagg, Dave 62
Fakava, Heikoti 62
Fambrough, Don 12
Fenderson, James 107
Fishback, Dick 6, 46
Fletcher, George 119
Fletcher, Nathan 57, 59, 109
Flores, Mike 18, 26, 30, 44
Flores, Quentin 52, 85, 96, 116
Freeman, Tom 17, 41
Freitas, Hartwell 6
Fryar, Irving 64, 83, 84, 86
Fry, Hayden 64, 87

G

Gabriel, Garrett 138
Gaison, Blane 4, 5, 6, 20, 24, 25, 29, 30, 36, 55, 59, 63, 70, 106, 107, 123, 133, 142, 145
Galimba, Raschad 96
Gardner, Mark 38
Garrett, Mike 66
Gearing, Vernon 74
Gibson, Mike 80
Gill, Eugene "Luke" 7
Gillman, Sid 10
Gill, Turner 83
Ginoza, Larry 59
Goeas, John 61
Goeas, Larry 60, 72, 82, 94, 99, 104, 121, 140
Goeas, Leo 61
Goodman, Curtis 23, 29, 30, 41, 43, 44, 47, 49
Gouveia, Kurt 59, 99
Gray, Riki 66
Green, Cornelius 23
Green, Darrell 21
Green, Dexter 32
Green, Gerald 29, 31, 43, 44, 48
Green, Jack 12
Griffith, Ben 127

H

Hall, Ron 33, 88, 95
Hallums, David 91
Hamilton, Waymon 93
Hanawahine, Bryan 23, 25, 44, 45, 67
Harbaugh, Jim 89, 118
Harbaugh, John 10
Harris, Vaness 44
Haslip, Wilbert 23, 29, 30, 31, 32, 43, 48, 56, 66, 67
Hata, Herbert 44
Hayes, Woody 10
Haynes, Mike 69
Heimuli, Lakei 99
Henry, Roy 32
Higa, Richard 106, 115
Hill, Keith 31, 41, 45, 70
Hill, Mike 83
Hill, Pat 130
Hinkle, Tony 9, 10
Hipp, Isaiah Moses 66
Hoffman, Al 109
Holmes, Dave 7, 17, 62, 82, 136
Holyfield, Tony 59, 82
Hubbard, Rudy 14, 16
Hudspeth, Max 29

J

Jackson, Mike 41, 43, 45, 66
Jackson, Reggie 69
Jacobs, Ron 2
James, Calvin 41
James, Don 16, 18
Jardine, Keoni 23, 31, 45, 48, 56
Jefferson, John 69
Jefferson, Thad 88
Jett, DeWayne 22, 32, 45, 71, 128
Johnson, Hank 10, 13
Johnson, Jimmy 10
Johnson, Lee 97
Johnson, Marco 78, 88, 96, 125, 141
Johnson, M.J. 88
Johnson, M.L. 60, 79, 95
Johnson, Paul 127, 139
Johnson, Sandra 141
Johnston, Chris 32, 66
Johnston, Russell 64
Jones, June 17, 43, 84, 86, 107, 108, 145
Jones, Lyndell 60

K

Kaʻaihue, Charlie 16, 42, 142
Kaʻaihue, Henry Kapono 17

Ka'aihue, Marmie 17
Ka'aihue, Ulu 17
Kafentzis, Kent 61, 62, 95–96, 113
Kafentzis, Kurt 61, 62
Kafentzis, Kyle 61
Kafentzis, Landon 61
Kafentzis, Mark 40, 61, 62, 72, 81, 106, 124
Kafentzis, Mikhail 61
Kafentzis, Sean 61
Kaftentzis, Tyson 61
Kahoano, Emlen "Embo" 52, 116, 124
Kalili, Jim 7
Kaloi, Alex 7, 22
Kamana, John 50
Kauahi, Kani 59, 82
Kaulukukui, Tommy 7
Kay, Doug 62, 95, 140
Kealoha, Beldon 32, 69
Keiter, Les 3, 109, 146
Kenneybrew, Carl 95
Kezirian, Ed 20, 58, 82
Killen, Shephard 97
Killen, Shepherd 117
Kim, Peter 59, 67
Klum, Otto "Proc" 6, 7
Knapp, Terrance 135
Knight, Tom 44
Knox, Chuck 18
Koga, Dave 97
Kozlowski, Glen 96
Kua, Stan 32
Kush, Frank 53, 69
Kwon, Bill 15
Kyle, Doug 40, 52, 81

L

Laboy, Cliff 7, 136
Laboy, Travis 107
Larsen, Don 8
Larsen, Lee 83, 93, 105

Leahey, Jim 88, 103, 108, 110, 127, 129
Lehor, Steve 59, 76, 121
Lewis, Ferd 68, 89
Little, Walt 29, 43, 56, 66
Lomax, Neil 44
Long, Chuck 87
Lopati, Junior 97, 104
Lopes, Merv 18, 82
Lord, Jack 28
Lott, Ronnie 64, 66, 68
Luck, Andrew 71
Luck, Oliver 71, 72
Lumpkin, George 17, 53, 54, 58, 62
Lum, Richard 28
Lutu, Leroy 50, 59
Lyons, Tim 75, 82, 93, 109

M

MacDuff, Larry 62, 124
Maeda, Nelson 56, 107
Malone, Mark 70
Mamiya, Hazel 50
Mamiya, Richard 50
Manumaleuna, Brandon 45
Manumaleuna, Frank 15, 44
Manumaleuna, John 45
Martin, Hubbard 47, 66
Mason, Tony 48
Matlin, David 145
Matsuda, Fujio 2
Matsushima, Harris 23, 30, 46, 48, 136
Mazzone, Noel 29
McBride, Ron 130
McClain, Dave 12
McCleod, Kingman 121
McDaniel, Dane 43
McElroy, Greg 32, 47, 66
McLemore, Dana 58, 82, 93, 109
McMackin, Greg 17, 130, 145
McMahon, Jim 75, 92, 93

Meyers, Georg N. 7
Miano, Rich 52, 74, 78, 94, 95, 106, 117, 128
Miller, Mark 45
Mills, Jim 82
Mokofisi, Filipo 86
Moku, Sam 104, 107, 125, 141
Mondt, Bill 29, 30
Montana, Joe 66
Moody, Andy 52, 59, 82, 93
Moon, Warren 72
Moore, Joe 109, 146
Mora, Jim 14, 16
Mora, Jim L. 14
Morgado, Arnold 7
Morrell, Kyle 96
Munoz, Anthony 66
Murakami, Les 8, 145
Murayama, Donna 8
Murphy, Tom 23, 42, 44, 46, 48
Murray, Walter ix, 54, 77, 84–85, 91, 94, 96, 97, 100, 117

N

Nagel, Ray 14, 21, 48, 129
Nakashima, Rick 103
Nielson, Gifford 32
Niumatalolo, Kenny 1, 138
Nobles, Joe 88
Noga, Al 61, 87, 88, 89, 95, 96, 137
Noga, Falaniko (Niko) 4, 50, 52, 61, 63, 73, 81, 97, 103, 109, 124, 137, 138, 140
Noga, Pete 61, 95, 137
Nomura, Doug 52
Norwood, Brian 52, 74
Nua, Mark 96

O

Odomes, Nate 64, 88
Ohira, Rod 30
Okazaki, Eric 92

Olds, Floyd 6
Onosai, Joe 87, 91, 96, 123, 125, 134
Osborne, Tom 64, 65, 83
Otto, Mike 44

P

Pager, Devah 128
Pangan, Carol 26
Panora, Joe 29, 66
Park, Kaulana 50
Parseghian, Ara 10
Paterno, Joe 17
Pavich, Mike 15
Payton, Sean 10
Pennick, Ron 82
Permetter, Coyle 89
Pont, John 10
Price, Larry 5, 6, 7, 14, 16, 17, 20, 21, 136
Proctor, Bobby 85

Q

Quarles, Bernard 55, 82, 83, 93, 94
Quina, Stan 32

R

Rakhshani, Steve 70
Randle, John 21
Reagan, Ronald 136
Redd, Verlon 59, 82, 128
Rhymes, George "Buster" 84
Rice, Grantland 7
Richards, Golden 7
Riewerts, Ed 81, 83, 108
Riggs, Gerald 70
Rimington, Dave 83
Rita, Adam 62
Robbins, Tony 26, 124–125
Robinson, Jerry 2
Robinson, John 64, 66, 68
Robinson, Reggie 82

Rodgers, Pepper 12, 13
Rogers, George 46
Rolovich, Nick 130, 145, 146
Rozier, Mike 64, 83

S

Saban, Nick 18
Salanoa, Thor 99
Santiago, Louis (Keala) 60, 116
Sapolu, Jesse 4, 52, 63, 65, 71, 81, 82, 93, 123, 139, 146
Sataua, Itai 59, 70
Satele, Alvis 52, 79, 87, 107, 124
Scanlan, Jerry 23, 29, 31, 32, 69
Schembechler, Glenn Edward "Bo" 10–13, 55, 64, 89, 120
Scherer, Rip 17, 19, 26
Schmidt, Pat 23, 30, 31, 44, 46, 48, 133
Scotts, Colin 60, 87, 96
Scullion, Kevin 32, 66
Seumalo, Joe 52
Sewak, Mike 127
Sheriff, Stan 102, 129
Sherrer, Larry 7, 32
Shoji, Dave 145
Sikahema, Vai 100
Simpson, O.J. 66
Sims, Marty 74
Sinclair, Steve 81
Slaughter, Webster 105, 141
Smith, Arthur 67
Smith, Dennis 66, 68
Smith, Homer 12, 13
Smith, Larry 10, 128
Souza, Bill 83
Spelman, Richard 85, 87, 96, 105, 117
Spotts, Gary 23, 30, 66
Stanley, Levi 7, 136
Steinkuhler, Dean 83
Stennis, Mike 32, 70, 71

Stringert, Hal 7
Stuprich, Reinhold 91
Switzer, Barry 64, 84

T

Talaesea, Junior 45, 51, 56, 67
Tanida, Edith 8
Tanuvasa, Maʻa 140
Tarver, Marcus 59, 82, 93
Tatsuno, Derek 8
Tatupu, Mosi 21, 57
Taylor, Charley 69
Taylor, John 60
Tillman, Spencer 84
Tipton, Gregg 88, 119
Tiumalu, Casey 95
Toloumu, David ix, 39, 56, 57–60, 62, 66, 67, 68, 70, 82, 93, 103, 146
Tomey, Angela 15, 100, 128
Tomey, Dale 8
Tomey, Lucille 8
Tomey, Marcia 8
Tomey, Rich 15, 40, 51, 110, 128
Tong, Sam 136
Tressel, Jim 10
Tuiasosopo, Manu 2, 15
Tuinei, Mark 59, 140, 143
Tuinei, Tom 17, 23, 43, 69, 104, 136, 142
Tuinei, Tumua 143
Tyler, Wendell 2

U

Ulufale, Semeri 56, 82
Upshaw, Gene 21
Ursery, Darryl 96, 116

V

Valverde, Rod 88
Van Horne, Keith 66, 104
Vasconcellos, Hank 6, 7

Vasconcellos, Mike 18
Veʻe-Noga, Taunuʻu 137, 138
Vermeil, Dick 12
Voeller, Scott 45, 67
von Appen, Fred 144

W

Wagner, Bob 16, 17, 18, 19, 48, 62, 74, 99, 101, 106, 127, 129, 138, 145, 146
Wagner, Rick 29, 41, 48
Walker, Elliot 32
Walker, Herschel 134
Walsh, Koldene 52
Waterhouse, Alec 100
Weathers, Robert 69
Weaver, Doug 12
White, Charles 64, 66, 67
White, Danny 69
White, Jeris 7
Whittingham, Fred 92
Whittingham, Kyle 92
Wilbur, John 18
Williams, Mike 29
Wilson, Artie 84
Wilson, Marc 91
Woodcock, John 7, 136
Woodson, Anthony 37, 75, 83
Wright, Jack 21, 32, 41, 47, 65, 68

Y

Yamaguchi, Andy 83
Yap, Boyd 50
Yee, Ben 79
Yee, Wadsworth 111
Young, Steve 91, 93, 94, 95, 96
Young, Vince 131

Z

Zornes, Dick 62

Dick Tomey was a college football head coach for twenty-nine seasons, including ten with the University of Hawai'i Rainbow Warriors. He is a former president of the American Football Coaches Association and currently chairs the Selection Committee of the Polynesian Football Hall of Fame. He and his wife, author Nanci Kincaid, reside in Tucson, Arizona.

Lance Tominaga is a Web Editor for ESPN 1420 Radio in Honolulu. He is a former magazine editor and has authored seven previous books, including *Catch the Dream: The Story of Hawaii Winter Baseball* and *The Hawaii Sports Trivia Challenge*.